W9-BUG-691

Special Places

On Cape Cod and the Islands

Special Places

On Cape Cod and the Islands

ROBERT FINCH

Illustrations by Ellen Raquel LeBow

Commonwealth Editions
Beverly, Massachusetts

Library of Congress Cataloging-in-Publication Data

Finch, Robert, 1943-

  Special places : on Cape Cod and the islands /
Robert Finch ; illustrations by Ellen Raquel LeBow.

      p. cm.

   ISBN 1-889833-51-7

   1. Cape Cod (Mass.)—Description and travel.
2. Martha's Vineyard (Mass.)—Description
and travel. 3. Nantucket Island (Mass.)—Description
and travel. 4. Natural areas—Massachusetts—Cape
Cod. 5. Natural areas—Massachusetts—Martha's
Vineyard. 6. Natural areas—Massachusetts—
Nantucket Island. 7. Cape Cod (Mass.)—Pictorial
works. 8. Martha's Vineyard (Mass.)—Pictorial
works. 9. Nantucket Island (Mass.)—Pictorial
works. I. Title.
  F72.C3 F566 2003

  917.44'920444—dc21   2002154257

Cover and interior design by Ann Conneman,
Peter King & Company.

Printed in Canada.

Published by Commonwealth Editions,
an imprint of Memoirs Unlimited, Inc.,
266 Cabot Street, Beverly, Massachusetts 01915.

Visit our Web site: www.commonwealtheditions.com.

Contents.

Acknowledgments.

I am grateful for all the help and assistance generously given to me by town employees, conservation commission members, conservation trust officials, and other private citizens dedicated to preserving open space on Cape Cod, Martha's Vineyard, and Nantucket. I would like to express particular thanks to Charles Merritt, Mario DeGregorio, John Cullity, Jim Freeborn, Bob Sherman, Ramona Peters, Peter Auger, Adam Gamble, Henry Kelley, Brian Malone, Margaret Swanson, Andy Young, Carol Spade, Dick Houghton, Henry Lind, Helen Purcell, Celine Gandolfo, Chris Egan, Jim Lantowski, and Peter Dunwiddie. I am especially pleased to have Ellen LeBow's superb interpretive illustrations grace this book.

Not Just Another Guide.

Why another guide to the Cape and Islands' natural areas, you might ask? And with reason. There have been numerous previous hiking, biking, canoeing, kayaking, automobile, and other guides, and more seem to appear each year. Hasn't this overvisited place already been signed, trailed, and interpreted to death? And if there are a few natural places left that have not been publicized to our annual hordes of visitors, why not leave them what small protection of anonymity that remains?

Well, to begin with, this is not a "guide" in the usual sense, so much as an introduction, such as one might make between mutual friends with the hope of encouraging deeper acquaintance. You will not find detailed trail directions here. If I am vague about the location of specific features, it is with the intent of encouraging self-exploration. If I seem overexplicit about the character of weather, light, or seasonal phenomena, it is to suggest that all of these places change on a seasonal, daily, even hourly basis. If my impressions and responses seem idiosyncratic, it is to suggest that all true natural experiences are personal and that my individual reactions are only one of an unlimited set of different experiences any of us may have in any of these places.

Inasmuch as it is a guide, this book is intended primarily for those of us who make our home here. It is local, in that it eschews the larger federal and state preserves—e.g., the Cape Cod National Seashore, Nickerson State Park—and instead concentrates on the smaller areas owned and managed by local conservation commissions or private conservation trusts. The pieces, which appeared in *Cape Cod Life* from 1999 to 2002, were written with an eye for focusing attention on the potential of the Cape Cod Land Bank Act, passed in November 1998, which authorized towns in Barnstable County to add a small surtax to local property bills to create a fund for acquiring local open space. (Martha's Vineyard and Nantucket had their own Land Banks approved several years before). Since then over 400 acres have been purchased using Cape Cod Land Bank funds.

The "places" in this book range from the 3,000-acre expanse of Barnstable's Sandy Neck to neighborhood "pocket parks" only a few acres in extent, and most are under 100 acres. They are "special," not so much in containing spectacular vistas or rare species and habitat (though many do), but for the often-unheralded role they play in enriching the quality of our daily lives here. Their value is that most are within walking distance of a good portion of the local populace, that they are representative rather than unusual landscapes, and that they therefore help to maintain the plants and animals characteristic of, though increasingly disappearing from, Cape Cod and the Islands.

As I look back over these pieces now, it seems to me that the most frequent message in them is that the landscapes of Cape Cod, Nantucket, and Martha's Vineyard (those parts, at least, which are not dominated by human constructs) are neither natural nor artificial, but rich amalgams and resultants of human and natural history. They have been shaped at times by the forces of nature—weather, glaciation, plant succession, animal migration, etc.—and at others by the forces of human alteration—settlement, agriculture, industry, transportation, recreation, etc. Whatever the balance, or whichever forces currently dominate, each place is but the present moment, a single page in an evolving drama of historical flux in which we can read elements of the past and indicators of the future if we know how to look. Seen this way, experienced carefully and with attention, these places are capable of telling us something about what we were, who we are, and where we might be going.

As for the protection of anonymity, that is a question all of us struggle with today. But over the years I have become convinced that even if anonymity is still possible on the Cape and Islands today, it is short-lived at best. In time all of our land's special places will be "discovered." Better to introduce them to those who would find them and try to convey their unique qualities, their vulnerability, and the potential rewards of approaching them with respect and patience.

Most of all, I hope that this book may encourage you to make your own discoveries in these special places.

Here and Nowhere Else.

Not long ago I attended an environmental conference in Boston. The theme was "biodiversity," a phrase that in the past decade has become a buzzword and a rallying cry for those trying to save the earth's endangered ecosystems and the diversity of life that depends upon them.

The loss of biodiversity is one of this planet's most critical—some would say the most critical—of our environmental problems, and it is always sobering to hear again the litany of the vast areas of habitat loss that take place each year and the accelerating rates of species extinction that accompany them.

I could not help but think, however, that when we speak about bio-diversity, we usually speak about threats to large-scale environ-ments, distant places and exotic species: ecosystems in Brazil rather than in Barnstable, the fragmentation of tropical rain forests rather than our local woodlands, the loss of the Sumatran rhinoceroses instead of local amphibians.

Important and overarching as these larger diversities are, I believe it is local diversity—that is, the small-scale and close-to-hand natural variety that we experience everyday—that determines our individual and personal sense of place, and that nourishes our commitment to larger goals.

When I speak of local diversity, I am talking not only about the dif-ferent species and habitats found in a small area such as Cape Cod, but also about the diversity within such an area, a recognition of the more subtle variations that define a single town, or even a neigh-borhood—those specific elements in our daily encounters with the local environment that give us a sense that we live, in the words of essayist Jane Brox, "here and nowhere else." In these articles, I wanted not only to spotlight local open spaces and to encourage the acquisition of more of them, but also to show how different they are from one another.

This is not a recognition that comes easily or quickly. Cape Cod is a region that is usually spoken of, even by year-round residents, as if it were one fairly homogeneous place, with bigger or smaller waves, and perhaps some variation in traffic from season to season. I have lived here for over thirty years, and I am still learning about local diversity. This was brought home to me several years ago when I moved from Brewster to Wellfleet. It was a move of only about 25 miles, but I was immediately aware, from my having lived so long and locally in one place, that I was now in another place, almost another country.

Take geology, for instance. Cape Cod, as almost everyone knows, is a glacially formed peninsula. In Brewster, however, there is an abundance of stone walls, and large boulders stud both the hills and the shoreline. One of its small rivers, Stony Brook, is even named after them. In Wellfleet, by contrast, there is a dearth of both stone walls and any stones to build them with, and only a few intertidal boulders. The difference is due to the fact that the Upper and Mid-Cape regions were formed by terminal and recessional moraines— that is, the leading or retreating edges of glaciers—which dumped numerous stones and boulders known as "glacial erratics" when they melted. The Outer Cape, by contrast, was formed by what is called an "interlobate moraine," or the side edges of two glacial lobes, which left relatively few erratics.

Even if I had not known of these geological differences, my arms would have recognized them when I came to dig my first Wellfleet garden. In contrast to the bone-jarring rocks my spade hit every spring in Brewster, digging in Wellfleet soil is like digging in pure sugar.

The different geology and geography of the two towns has resulted in another kind of local diversity. Wellfleet's soil is much sandier and lighter than Brewster's, which contains large amounts of clay. This, in turn, has contributed to different forest types in the two places. Like most of New England, the Cape was stripped of its original woodlands fairly early, and its recovery has been slower than in inland areas. In most Cape towns oaks are now the dominant trees. On the Outer Cape, however, where the soil is sandier and poorer, and where salt winds blow in more heavily from the Atlantic, the salt-resistant pitch pine has remained dominant.

Looking more closely, one can see how these differences in soil types have produced even more specific differences in forest cover across the Cape. On the Upper Cape, for instance, one finds numerous large stands of holly, white pine, beech, and even some hemlock—species which grow more scarce as one moves east and which, with a few exceptions, are practically nonexistent below Orleans.

Not all local diversity is so simply explained. For instance, there is an extraordinary abundance of red cedar trees (actually a juniper) in East Orleans and the southern portions of Eastham. Red cedars are usually a sign of abandoned pastures, but I have yet to find a satisfactory explanation of why they are so abundant in these specific areas.

Just as geology and geography produce local diversity in flora, so floral diversity in turn produces a host of differences in the kinds of animals found in different parts of the Cape, especially birds. I'll mention only two examples. There are fewer screech owls on the Outer Cape than in the Upper and Mid-Cape areas, for these birds prefer mature deciduous woods, where hollow trunks provide nests for them. On the other hand, in Wellfleet I occasionally hear the uncommon and peculiar call of the saw-whet owl (its call resembles the sound of a saw being sharpened, hence its name), our smallest owl and one which nests in pine woods. For the same reason, I see fewer ruffed grouse (for whom acorns are a main food source) in Wellfleet than I did in Brewster. But I also hear more whippoor-wills, which prefer unbroken pine woods (though sometimes, at 2 A.M., for instance, I'm not sure it's a blessing).

The same kind of local diversity found on land is also found along and off our shorelines. The curving hook of Cape Cod diverts the warm Gulf Stream away from our northern coast, creating a differ-ence of several degrees in the mean temperature of the waters on the northern and southern sides of the peninsula. Because of this, many common marine species reach the limits of their ranges at Cape Cod.

If I were blindfolded and set down on a local beach or salt marsh, the salt water community would give me several hints as to what side of the Cape I was on. If I saw blue crabs, for instance, I would be pretty sure I was on an estuary of Nantucket Sound, Buzzards Bay, or Pleasant Bay, for these southern crabs prefer warmer waters. On the other hand, the presence of waved whelks (whose rounded, grayish masses of small, transparent egg sacs are frequently found by beach-strollers) would be a clue that I was on the Cape's northern shore, for these gastropods favor the colder, littoral waters of Cape Cod Bay.

Sometimes these local environmental differences have personal, even gastronomical, consequences. One autumn ritual I always looked forward to in Brewster was going out onto the tidal flats to gather quahogs. Brewster has the largest expanse of tidal flats of any town on the East Coast, in some places extending over a mile at low tide. Wellfleet, on the other hand, has a much smaller area of flats, and many fewer quahogs. It does, however, have oysters, and with a $25 resident shellfish permit I can pick up ten quarts of Wellfleet's finest every week during the season. Compared to the long trek and arduous work involved in scratching for quahogs, the gathering of oysters is so easy it almost seems like cheating. This difference is due to a number of environmental factors in confluence, including the particular composition of the mudflats on which the oysters grow and the infusion of fresh water from Wellfleet's Herring River, which creates the peculiar chemistry of the local brackish marine environment that oysters seem to love.

Even within the rather limited range of oyster habitats on Cape Cod, there appears to be significant diversity. There are those who claim palates sophisticated enough to be able to distinguish the taste of Wellfleet oysters from those grown in, say, Cotuit, much as some wine connoisseurs are said to be able to identify a bottle of fine Bordeaux not only as coming from a particular town, but even from a particular vineyard, recognizing the individual environment in the taste of the grape. I have not yet lived long enough in Wellfleet and tasted enough oysters to have developed this ability, but I intend to keep trying.

Such examples of local diversity could be multiplied almost endlessly, and the articles that follow provide further illustrations found in the Cape and Islands' own special places. But the point I want to make here is that cultivating a recognition of local diversity, in all its varied natural facets, not only adds to the pleasure of living in a particular locale (which it certainly does), but also, I believe, helps to preserve the places where we live.

In his essay "The American Geographies," Barry Lopez talks about the danger of losing the reality of local diversity to what he calls the "myth of a national geography." Politicians and corporations, he argues, want us to believe that "there can be a national geography because [then] the constituent parts are interchangeable and can be treated as commodities." The vast complexity and diversity of the American landscape, he says, tends to be represented in the media merely as "attractive scenery," as "an incomplete or even spurious geography as an inducement to purchase a unique experience."

This has certainly been true here, where "the Cape Cod experience" has been marketed relentlessly, to the detriment of what is actually here. That is one reason why I have tried to focus, in treating the areas in this book, on the depth of differences, the innumerable details of local landscapes that distinguish one from the other and which, cumulatively, define the true Cape and Islands. I believe that this is one of the most important tasks for those who care about the local environment: to help reclaim the intricacy, reality, and infinite distinctions of individual places from the oversimplifications and distortions of those who see land primarily as commodity. For if we lose a sense of the true complexity and diversity of our own home grounds, we will more easily buy into the commercial and political concepts of our environment, which will in turn lead us to more readily accept public policies and commercial exploitation geared to turn every place into Anyplace USA. And if we lose sight of our home ground, how can we hope to see, much less save, the earth itself?

A Rich Neighbor.

FALMOUTH'S BEEBE WOODS LIE ALONG THE CREST of the Buzzards Bay moraine, the highest, hilliest, and rockiest of the three glacial moraines, or strings of low hills, that form the "backbone of Cape Cod." Large boulders, many of them larger than elephants, are planted throughout its hills, the legacy of a vast, vanished, glacial flow whose massive icy head traveled 3,000 miles south from the Labrador Canadian Shield, planing and leveling with immense forces the once towering Appalachian Mountain Range to leave its mark as a terminal ridge of rock and glacial till. It is here, more than anywhere else on this shifting, changing piece of land, that one can get a feeling of stability and solidity, of being inland instead of at sea.

The story of the Beebe Woods and how it came to be preserved as a "public park" is a fascinating tale that was recounted with rare narrative flare by George Moses in his 1976 book, *Ring Around the Punch Bowl,* now unfortunately out of print. It is a story whose elements figure in the history of many public preserves in Massachusetts: a private nineteenth-century estate owned by a wealthy Bostonian (James M. Beebe) and kept from development by his descendants for generations; threats of sale, fragmentation, and development in the 1960s; and a last-minute act of public philanthropy. In the case of the Beebe Woods, the philanthropists were Mr. and Mrs. Josiah K. Lilly III of the famous pharmaceutical family, who in 1972 bought the old Beebe estate from Highfield Associates for just over $2 million and gave 390 acres of ponds and forest to the town as a wild park for the "quiet enjoyment of the land." (A subsequent purchase of ten acres by the town in 1984 protects the north shore of Deep Pond.) The Lillys' generosity was one of the last of many such acts of land philanthropy, the kind of gift we can no longer rely on to preserve our landscape, but whose legacy we continue to enjoy and whose spirit we should, as communities, emulate.

As you approach the Beebe Woods from the formal entrance drive, the grounds around the old Highfield mansion,* the Highfield Theatre, and the Cape Cod Conservatory form an interesting introduction and contrast to the extensive forest beyond. The lawns are dominated by large trees alien to this area, human imports. Massive European weeping beeches with drooping canopies shade lush patches of Solomon's seal. European elms, red pines, sweet gum, tulip trees, larch, and sugar maples grow here to cultivated dimensions that our native trees rarely attain. In addition, there are a couple of enormous specimen American beeches, six or seven feet in diameter, whose trunks resemble the fused forms of human torsos. Songbirds find such a transitional setting attractive: yellowthroats chant from the bushes, robins and cowbirds probe and graze on the lawn, a yellow-tailed flicker cackles from a nearby pine.

* Since this essay was written, the town of Falmouth has acquired the old mansion, and the building and grounds are being restored by a volunteer, nonprofit group, Historic Highfield, Inc.

Beyond the immediate setting of the old mansion, the Highfield Theatre and the Cape Cod Conservatory, there is evidence that human influence was once wider here, and that the woods have begun to reclaim their own. Not far from the parking lot there is an old, abandoned apple orchard, where in autumn the trees hang out their tart misshapen fruit while heaps of wild grapes wind about them. On the edges of the grounds are the remains of a large, once-elegant greenhouse. Here, where geraniums and pansies were once carefully nurtured and tended, beds of dandelions, blackberry vines, and Virginia creeper now flourish among the rotting wooden trays, rusted hot-water pipes and radiators, and shards of broken glass. The sun streams through the empty rib-work of the roof, and a single female catbird keeps noisy vigil, warning the intruder off from a nest she has hidden somewhere among the ruins.

If the grounds are exotic, the forest itself is fairly typical of the Cape's morainal woodlands. The trees are predominantly second-growth mixed black and white oak, most less than 60 or 70 years old, sprouts of trees killed in a vast fire that swept through most of the tract in 1947. But look more closely and you can find occasional black locusts, tupelo, grey birch, hemlock, poplar, red cedar, black cherry, holly, and, in isolated spots, flowering dogwood.

At the entrance to the woods are impressive stands of white pines, some over two feet in diameter. At a bend in one of the old carriage roads that wind through the woods, two large old pine trunks, felled by some forgotten storm — perhaps the legendary 1938 hurricane — lie together in stranded majesty like huge twin skeletons of beached whales. They have, in fact, the color and crumbly texture of old whale bones found on the beach. Their long spires, still intact and lichen-encrusted, point due northwest, recording like frozen weathervanes the fate that rushed in from the southeast to fell them many decades ago.

There are, as well, substantial groves of native beech, a tree uncommon on most of Cape Cod that favors these rocky, hilly areas. Beeches take strange forms; one not too far in is a "Siamese beech," a tree whose trunk splits at the base and then rejoins some eight or nine feet off the ground.

In deep woods, spring flowers are not generally abundant, but the forest here has an unusual number of at least two plants that are considered uncommon in most of Massachusetts. In late April and early May the tree-lined paths and roads give off the subtle sweet fragrance of our state flower, trailing arbutus or mayflower. Large mats of this low, leathery-leafed plant line the slopes and the road banks, cradling their small, white, fragrant flowers. In late May and June large numbers of pink lady's-slippers, or moccasin orchids, raise their showy raspberry heads, sometimes in crowds of a hundred or more. Though numerous here, both of these plants are protected and should not be picked.

By late spring the leaves are out in full and the bird population, though large, is more often heard than seen. The muted calls of mourning doves, titmice, ovenbirds, towhees, chipping sparrows, cardinals, yellow warblers, chickadees, flickers, goldfinches, quail, redwings, and nuthatches filter through the fresh new greenery and perennial latticework of branches, and the drumming of a male grouse on his courting ground booms faintly like disappearing thunder somewhere in the distance.

Covered with a hard clayey soil and carpeted with a thick forest of oak, pine, and beech, this forest creates a feeling of peace and calm, of persisting forms. The woods are solid, firm, unyielding, and comparatively immobile. Here energy is held captive, molded into form: the trees themselves are living fossils of sunlight, air, and water, trapped into rigid unmoving forms that slowly spread their canopies and extend root systems to bind the hills and ravines into even more enduring shapes. Among the trees motion is, for the most part, furtive and unseen, or at a pace below human perception.

Here in this wooded heart lies the centerpiece of the Beebe Woods: Deep Pond, a pristine three-acre pond cupped in the bottom of a steep kettle hole. It is surrounded by steep 70-foot high slopes that radiate up and out in a nearly perfect geological formation that inspired the aristocratic Beebes to rename it "The Punch Bowl." Nearly every Cape town has its Deep Pond or No Bottom Pond. Perhaps the early Cape settlers, lacking mountainous heights, sought with such names to confer distinction upon the land's invisible depths. Usually, though, these bodies of water prove not only to have bottoms, but relatively shallow ones at that.

Nonetheless, I had heard that the Punch Bowl was truly deep and had, in fact, been sounded at 200 feet. Though skeptical, I set off one summer day for the Punch Bowl carrying an inflatable rubber

DIRECTIONS

From Palmer Avenue
(Route 28) in
Falmouth center, turn
onto Depot Avenue,
go across the railroad
tracks, and continue
up Highland Avenue
to the parking lot
between the Highfield
Theater and the Cape
Cod Conservatory. The
entrance to the Beebe
Woods is directly to
the right of the con-
servatory. A walking
map of the area,
made by students at
the nearby Falmouth
Academy, is available
at the Conservation
Commission office in
Town Hall Square off
Main Street in
Falmouth.

kayak, an old lead window weight, and a length of line to determine its profundity for myself. I descended the sides of the kettle hole to its sparkling waters, where a kingfisher announced my arrival, swooping over the pond with his machine-gun rattle. Swallows dipped and dove above the surface, plucking summer insects out of the air, while water striders and whirligigs performed their surface-tension acrobatics, for nobody's pleasure in particular.

As I set off from shore, the overhead breeze dipped low, scattering arpeggios across the pond's sunken surface. Then it passed and was replaced again by unruffled calm. I took eight different soundings at various points and was somewhat disappointed, though not really surprised, to find that its maximum depth was a modest 13 feet.

So it seemed that the myth of Deep Pond was a shallow one. I had to conclude that the steep sides of the kettle hole were misleading and that the Punch Bowl was, in fact, a rather uniform, shallow, and somewhat eutrophic pond. Was its original name, then, just an expression of wishful thinking? Was it perhaps named after some early settler - Obadiah Deep? Or did some cautious pioneer mother give it that misleading name to keep her children away from it?

Most likely, of course, the name reflects not the depth of the pond itself, but rather its deep setting, some 70 feet below the circling ridges, making it look as if it *ought* to be deep. And deep it is, despite my literal soundings. Set like a hidden jewel in the very heart of the Beebe Woods, the Punch Bowl symbolizes perfectly the unfathomable loveliness of the woods and the unending layers of life of the surrounding hills mirrored upwards from its waters.

Despite such unusual formations and features as the Punch Bowl, however, the real value of the Beebe Woods, to my mind, is that it is not special, but representative. It is a genuine piece of our Cape Cod forests today (albeit a remarkably large and intact piece). Its trees are common trees, its associations natural ones. Its branches and waters are threaded with our characteristic birds, animals, and insects. Its seasons are our seasons. It is part and parcel of the land in which it sits, and it reflects the life of this besieged peninsula.

In this anonymous richness lies its true legacy and enduring poten-tial. We can enter the woods, not to see strange sights and unusual creatures, but to know our land and, thereby, ourselves. It draws added value from being in such close proximity to one of the most urbanized areas in Barnstable County. Literally across the street from downtown Falmouth, this 400-acre "park" looms above the town with a potential influence such as the Beebes themselves, in all their baronial splendor, never possessed. It sits in protected juxtaposition to the habitations of men and women, offering a form of improvement and development too little regarded in our real estate age, a fund from which all people may borrow and invest at no interest, creating instead its own interest compounded annually from the bright fallen coins of its leaves.

With such a generous and cooperative neighbor next door, who can say what salutary changes might occur in our own lives? Who knows but what, with such opportunities so close at hand, we may some day learn to live, not merely next to, but with our natural surroundings?

New Life for an Old Farm.

I FIRST CAME UPON THE BOURNE FARM OVER

20 years ago while bicycling through West Falmouth one October

afternoon. At that time the farm had an abandoned look, although

there were still a few horses grazing in the pasture behind the barn.

A dead elm leaned precariously over the ancient, badly peeling

farmhouse, the stone doorstep was covered with ivy, and a knock

brought no reply from inside. Behind the house was a ragged series

of deserted outbuildings, all covered with wild bittersweet vines

unpeeling their brilliant autumn fruit. The fields beyond were

unmown and overgrown with milkweed, chicory, and goldenrod,

and several rusted junk cars lay beside the back stone wall.

This was during the development boom of the late 1970s, and I assumed that this farm would shortly suffer the fate of almost all small farms on the Cape, and that its last crop would be subdivision houses. So I was pleased to be proved wrong when in 1979 the Salt Pond Areas Bird Sanctuaries, Inc., a private conservation organization in Falmouth, acquired the 33-acre property from the Bourne family and proceeded to restore the farmhouse and outbuildings. Recently the organization purchased an additional parcel, bringing the total to 49 acres and creating a wildlife corridor that connects with the town-owned Wing's Pond conservation property to the north.

I revisited the farm last June on a gorgeous early summer's day, the sun bright and warm, the air cool and dry, with a light breeze rustling the new leaves. The 2½-story 1775 farmhouse and the large barn behind it have been impeccably restored. A lovely grape arbor has been established next to the house, with granite picnic tables and benches beneath it. More stonework has been built or restored on the grounds: a circular stone wall faces the south side of the barn, and other walls follow the sloping grassy hillside that leads down to Crocker Pond, a lovely kettle-hole pond with thickly vegetated borders. The grounds immediately around the farmhouse and barn are so entrancing, in fact, that one is almost tempted to go no farther.

Although there is no longer any livestock, the SPABS keeps the property as a "working farm." There are extensive herb gardens and more grape arbors planted around the farm buildings. On the west slope of the pond is a small apple orchard, and in the open, mowed field are irrigated rows of pumpkin vines, which the organization sells at its annual Columbus Day weekend Pumpkin Day event.

It is all almost a little too perfect, the way such well-done restorations tend to be. It is doubtful any of these old farms were quite so meticulously and neatly maintained; subsistence rarely gave priority to aesthetics. Bourne Farm has been frozen in time, perhaps even pushed back a little in time, to be an exhibit, a museum display of an old Cape Cod farm. But given the alternatives (subdivision, golf course, office park), I find it hard to quibble with the unnatural perfection of such careful preservation.

Perhaps the most remarkable thing about the property is the scene it presents from the highway: that of a large open field, a sight that has become increasingly rare on the Cape. As I walked out into the

old hay pasture, a meadowlark flew up in front of me, reminding me that, as fields have disappeared, so have many local species, including such open-ground nesters as meadowlarks, bobolinks, and upland sandpipers, not to mention many native wildflowers.

But Bourne Farm has its own individual character, or look, as well: the open, slightly undulating field stretches for several hundred feet toward the rear where it is bordered by a long stone wall. Behind the wall a heavily forested hillside climbs up above the surrounding plain. This is the classic landscape of a hill farm in inland Massachusetts, or the lower parts of New Hampshire or Vermont. The hill behind the field is an outrider spur of the much higher Buzzards Bay moraine that lies east of the farm. Though the hill rises only to just under 100 feet, it dominates the outwash plain surrounding it.

I followed the dirt road to the back of the field where several hand-lettered "Nature Trails" signs pointed me to a break in the stone wall. The stones in the wall are hernia-sized glacial erratics, averaging two feet across. Oxen may have dragged them down from the hills, but men still had to leverage them into place. One trail off to the left goes through a dense grove of tall spiraling spruces where the air is noticeably cooler. The dark, hushed understory of the grove reminds me of historian Simon Schama's contention that the Gothic cathedrals of Germany and France were inspired by the dark firs and spruces of the Black Forest. Then the trail suddenly emerges into a space of blinding light: a small meadow full of buttercups, thistles, ox-eye daisies, and some small white wild roses.

The trail to the right climbs up the hill into the forest behind the fields. Although this is now a mature forest of mostly oak and some pine, the presence of several large old "wolf trees" (wide-spreading oaks so called by foresters because they "wolf" the sunlight from other trees) suggests that this was previously open pasture. If one squints one can almost see the ghosts of cows that once chewed their cud beneath the shade of these old spreading oaks.

The undergrowth here is typical — some white pine, holly, catbrier, huckleberry, sassafras. The trail loops and winds up the slopes and around mini-kettle holes. Here the hillside is dotted with large, lichen-encrusted boulders left by the great ice-contact sheet that sculpted these hills 20,000 years ago, and which likely provided the granite for the profuse stonework on the farm.

DIRECTIONS

Bourne Farm is located on the west side of the West Falmouth Highway (Route 28A) at the intersection with Thomas Landers Road. From the Bourne Bridge rotary, take Route 28 south for 10.25 miles to the Thomas Landers Road exit and go west 0.125 mile. From Falmouth center take Route 28 north for 4.5 miles to the same exit. The grounds are open to the public during daylight hours.

But what overwhelmingly captures the eye this time of year — the unexpected, incredible gift of this place during mid-June to late July — is the proliferation of flowering mountain laurel: fountains of milky white and pink-tinged blossoms gushing up to eight feet high beneath the dark shade of these woods. Although these plants are not commonly found growing wild on the Cape (preferring the rockier soils of inland areas), their abundance and ubiquity at first suggested that they were native shrubs that had found a particularly congenial mix of acid soil, shade, and moisture in which to thrive on this abandoned hillside. I later found out that they were, in fact, planted through the generosity and under the direction of the late Ermine Lovell, founder of the Salt Pond Areas Bird Sanctuaries. At any rate, their seasonal luxuriance is a fitting memorial to her, and in all its long history, it is unlikely that this farm ever raised such a lush bumper crop as these blossoming June laurels.

Finally, reaching the northern end of these woods, I descended onto the old Penn Central Railroad track, now abandoned, that parallels the stone wall at the back of the fields. Its rails are still intact, but rusted over and partially obscured by tall grasses growing on the bed. As I walked along the track I came upon what is probably the most singular feature of the entire property: a short cattle chute, or tunnel, perhaps 20 feet in length, that goes beneath the track. The farm preceded the railroad by a century or more, and the tunnel was obviously built to allow the cows safe access from the barn to the hillside pasture. (It was not for nothing that the iron skirts that used to be on the fronts of locomotives were known as "cow catchers.")

The tunnel is low and narrow, barely three feet wide, effectively limiting the size of the cattle that could pass through it. (One could see it as a cautionary fable about greed: eat too much and you were forced to go over the tracks, thus risking being turned into instant cowburger.) I stepped off the track and followed the old cow path down beneath the bed where, stooping, I entered the tunnel. Its walls and low ceiling are constructed of large, roughly squared granite blocks. Though short, it is remarkably dark, cool, and perpetually moist inside. I wondered if the cows ever lumbered through here as a train was passing over. What a tumultuous thundering they must have experienced — enough, perhaps, to have curdled their milk!

At present there are no scheduled tours of the farmhouse, but a series of summer nature programs geared for children and families is offered in July and August. The annual Pumpkin Day event is held on the Saturday of Columbus Day weekend. The grounds are also available for weddings and other formal events. For further information, call the Salt Pond Areas Bird Sanctuaries, Inc., at 508-548-8484.

As my eyes began to adjust to the darkness, I saw that several spiders were still making a living along the damp walls of this tunnel — no longer in danger of having their webs scraped off the stones by a passing side of beef. And then, as my pupils further enlarged, I saw another, unexpected sign of nature's unrelenting multiple use policy, her faculty and inventiveness for using and reusing man's abandoned artifacts for her own needs. Attached to both sides of the tunnel's walls were a half dozen or so squat, cone-shaped nests made of mud and grass. There were no birds in sight, and the nests were too close to the ceiling of the tunnel for me to look into them; but I reached up and gently felt over the rim of one, where my fingers touched four or five small, round, delicate, perfect barn swallow eggs.

A Presidental Retreat, an Evolving Landscape.

As I POINT OUT ELSEWHERE IN THIS BOOK,

virtually every piece of open space on Cape Cod exhibits signs of

previous human alteration. In the case of the Four Ponds

Conservation Area in Bourne, however, this discrepancy between the

"natural" appearance of the area and the depth and intensity of

human history hidden within it is unusual even for the Cape. It is a

history that includes, among other things, an active chapter in the

Industrial Revolution, an exclusive private sportsmen's club, a

nationwide egg business, and visits from two U.S. Presidents.

None of this is obvious as you enter the cool and shadowy woods of this 133-acre park. The rush and hum of summer traffic on the bordering roads recedes into the hush of tall pines, dense oaks, and great bunches of red maple trunks that sprout out of the ground like giant bouquets. The terrain is quite hilly, the paths paved with soft pine needles, and there are inviting benches spaced out along the trails. The eponymous "Four Ponds" — Upper Pond, Freeman Pond, The Basin, and Shop Pond — are strung along the course of a clear stream that runs from east to west, like sparkling sapphires on a thin blue string. They are modest-sized but exquisitely lovely waterbodies, seemingly pristine and untouched.

Soon, however, you begin to notice things that suggest this place may have been shaped, at least in part, by human hands. For one thing, the paths around the ponds are built up with fairly elaborate rock walls, suggesting a purpose more pragmatic than a conservation area. There are dirt dikes separating some of the ponds, and near them the overgrown cuts, or "barrows," in the hillside, which were probably excavated to make them. Also, the course of the flow between the ponds seems artificially complex. The outlet from Freeman Pond, for instance, runs due west several hundred feet, where it meets the outflow from The Basin and then zigzags sharply to the east. It reminds you of the kind of "rustic" stream systems Frederick Law Olmsted designed for some of his nineteenth-century city parks.

Then, on a bluff above Freeman Pond, you come upon a curious concrete slab, maybe 20 by 35 feet, littered with glass and flowering weeds. At one end is the ruined stone base of a hearth and chimney. But it has no signs of an old homestead — there are no lilacs or planted trees, no root cellar, nothing that would suggest former permanent habitation. What was this?

These are some of the mute signs of a long history of human habitation and alteration of this area, going back at least to the early days of the Republic. It is the story, not of a single master designer, but of the evolving uses we have made of, and the changing attitudes we have had toward, the Cape's landscape over past generations.

Around 1800, when this area was a part of Sandwich, none of these ponds existed. Instead, it was the upper course of the Pocasset River, a small stream that drained an extensive swamp to the east and flowed west into Buzzards Bay. By the 1820s, however, what

now serves as a secluded nature preserve was a bustling industrial center, containing a mill, an iron foundry and a blacksmith shop (source of the name "Shop Pond"). To service and power these enterprises, wells were dug into the swamp at the head of the stream to increase its flow, and a series of six linked ponds were created as reservoirs. (Two additional ponds, Lower and Mill, lie to the west of Four Ponds.)

By the late 1880s the ponds and surrounding land (now part of the new town of Bourne) were bought by Stephen M. Weld, a brigadier general in the Civil War, who, with several other friends, formed the Tahanto Fishing Club, whose lodge stood on that concrete slab above Freeman Pond. The ponds, stocked with brook and rainbow trout, attracted many notable guests over the years, including Presidents Grover Cleveland and Calvin Coolidge. (One of my favorite Cape Cod stories, told by Josef Berger in his 1937 book, *Cape Cod Pilot,* concerns President Cleveland, whose summer home, Grey Gables, stood only a few miles away. The story is that one day, while out fishing in the Sandwich woods, Cleveland became lost. He eventually came upon an old Cape house and knocked on the door. After repeated knockings, the sash in an upper window went up and an old man leaned out and demanded, "What do y' want?" "I'm the President of the United States," Cleveland replied," and I'd like to stay here tonight." "Well then," the man replied, "Stay there!" And down went the sash.)

In the early 1900s an extensive system of trout hatchery pools was established in the swamp above Upper Pond. So successful was the hatchery that not only did it supply the Four Ponds with trout, but trout eggs, packed in trays lined with sphagnum moss and covered with ice, were shipped by freight trains all over the country.

The commercial hatchery closed in 1934, but the private club continued until the late 1960s. In 1983 the residents of Bourne acquired the property for conservation. In a cooperative venture between public and private organizations, the area is now managed by the Bourne Conservation Commission and maintained by the Volunteers of the Bourne Lions Club and local Eagle Scouts, who built the linked system of trails and installed benches along the paths. To the north, Four Ponds is abutted by an additional 312 acres of town forest and water district land, which are also open to hiking.

On the summer day I visited the area, I started at the eastern end of the ponds, walking downstream. Above Upper Pond is a swampy area of meandering sloughs and moss-covered hummocks that must have been where the hatchery pools were built. Now it had the look of a tropical forest, with thick growth sprouting out of dead, fallen, and half-submerged trees.

Upper Pond itself is a thin, narrow pond. Swimming in the shallows along its shores that day were schools of tiny apostrophe-shaped herring fry, indicating that a natural alewife run has replaced the artificially stocked trout. Many of the trees in this woodland are impressive in size and appearance. Next to the dike separating Upper and Freeman Ponds is the granddaddy of all the white pines in this area — a rugged, hoary tree over three feet in diameter, rising undiminished from the ground to a height of eight or nine feet. At this point the trunk branches out into a candelabrum of large black limbs over a foot thick (suggesting insect or lightning damage) that rise 60 feet or more into the air, forming a light-green heaven of feathery needles. This tree must be nearly two centuries old, a witness to most of the changes this area has seen. It seemed to invite me to sit beneath its massive branches and listen to the stories it had to tell.

Not too far from this pine I came upon a large red maple. In the side of its trunk at about chest height was an old wound full of rotting sawdust, and at the base of the wound was an incredibly bright, sun-yellow fungus. It was a type of shelf fungus, in the shape of mitts for truncated hands, covered with various warts. In the cups of these miniature mitts were tiny, shining pools of recent rain, over which bright green flies were swarming, as though they sensed something sweet or decaying in it.

The second pond, Freeman Pond, is the largest, perhaps 200 yards long and fish-shaped in outline. A pair of mute swans was feeding on its eastern end, their large white bodies upended, their long necks and heads submerged, so that they looked like small icebergs floating in the pond.

As I walked along its banks, I heard a small rustle in the dead leaves, and then a tiny snapping turtle came waddling toward the pond. It was only about four inches long, but its large, black, death's-head eyes already had a fearless gaze about them. There was a large leech attached to its rear plate. It did not shrink into its shell as I approached. It was not afraid of me. It already knew it will grow up to be something formidable, something that might even take one of those swans some day.

At the outlet of Freeman Pond I was startled by some young teenagers in camouflage fatigues carrying what looked like air rifles. Then I realized that they were playing paintball. But they politely called a cease-fire and let me pass unstained. I suspect this activity may be illegal here, and in any case reprehensible to many minds, but I found myself thinking, Are these boys any more mischievous or predatory than the rich sportsmen and politicians that hunted and fished here a century ago?

Between Freeman Pond and The Basin (so-called for its round shape and surrounding hills) there is a small cattail swamp. The thick sweet smell of white pepperbush blossoms growing along its edge made me dizzy. Also called Indian soap-bush, sweet pepper-bush flowers, if rubbed between wet hands, work up into a fragrant lather. On the far side of the pond, the bent-wing form of an osprey, looking as large as an eagle on this small pond, lifted off a pine branch and dropped to the water surface, rising again with a large perch in its talons.

Near the outflow of The Basin I found a profuse stand of jewel-weed, or touch-me-not, whose bright yellow blossoms were grow-ing, as they often do, right next to poison ivy, for which the crushed juice of jewelweed is an effective salve. Continuing west, I followed the stream as it gradually widened out into the elongated, tadpole-shaped form of the last of the Four Ponds, Shop Pond. Here I emerged from the deep shade of the forest into the bright summer sun, along a path lined with mounds of bittersweet, grapes, chokecherries, and dried grass heads as high as my chest. In places the vines had buried entire trees, so that one could hardly tell what they had been. Here and there branches of cedar peeked out from the enshrouding vines, like corners of Mayan temples in the Yucatan jungle.

The pond, and the conservation area, stop at a dam formed by County Road at its western end. Long tresses of waterweeds waved in the shimmering water, with schools of small minnows swimming in front of it. Suddenly a large pickerel, maybe 16 to 18 inches long, swirled up from the depths, scattering the minnows.

DIRECTIONS

A color-coded map of the Four Ponds Conservation Area (highly recommend-ed) is available at the Bourne Conservation Commission office at Bourne Town Hall, 24 Perry Street, or by calling 508-759-0625. The main entrance to the area is on the north side of Barlows Landing Road, 0.8 mile west of the Barlows Landing Road exit off Route 28 (3.3 miles south of the Bourne Bridge rotary at the canal), or 0.25 mile east of County Road.

All in all, I spent only an hour or so — although a very rich hour — in this area now known as Four Ponds. It was an hour not just in a year of daily and seasonal changes, but in a long and unfinished history in which we and our predecessors have played varied and changing roles. I could not help but wonder, would I recognize this place in another 200 years? What will it be called then? Will the Four Ponds still exist, or will their artificial impoundments have vanished, reinstating the original stream? And most of all, I wondered what, if anything, will visitors in the year 2200 A.D. detect of our presence here today?

For historical information about the Four Ponds Conservation Area, the author is indebted to an article by Alice M. Gibbs of the Bourne Archives Committee.

Harleys and Herring.

ALONG THE CAPE COD CANAL IN BOURNE, ABOUT

a mile west on Route 6 from the Sagamore Bridge rotary, the

Bournedale herring run, one of the largest alewife runs on Cape

Cod, enters from the canal through a series of concrete fish ladders,

goes under the highway, and emerges next to the Herring Run Motel

into what looks very much like a swimming pool. For years I had

wondered about this seemingly improbable arrangement, so one day

last spring I stopped at the motel to investigate. I found chairs

placed around the pool and signs that read "No Lifeguard on Duty —

Swim at Own Risk — No Diving." The pool was black with swarming

alewives who didn't seem worried about the lack of a lifeguard and

certainly didn't seem to be trying to dive.

The motel was not open for the season yet, but I talked to the manager and asked him what the story was.

The motel, he said, had been there for about 50 years and, yes, the pool had been used as a swimming area for the motel guests until recently. "They didn't use it until after the spawning season was over in late May, but now the town doesn't allow people to swim there because it doesn't meet health regulations. You can't chlorinate it, you see, because it's part of a state fishway. It's not really a pool, though. It's got a dirt bottom. It's really just a widening in the stream. It's too bad — people used to enjoy it. People have been using this area for centuries. The Indians camped here during the run and caught herring in their nets."

As far as I know, this is the only herring run on Cape Cod, perhaps in all of New England, that had an active swimming pool as part of its ecosystem. But multiple use on this site goes back a long way. Above the pool another series of smaller fish ladders runs in back of a line of motel cabins and climbs into a small pond known as Foundry Pond. Apparently, in the late nineteenth century, this area was a small hub of industrial and commercial activity. The 1880 Atlas of Barnstable County shows two iron foundries, a stable, a train depot, a shop, and a "Tenement Hospital" on or near the site of the present motel. At that time, of course, there was no Cape Cod Canal and no town of Bourne. The herring followed the Monument River up from Buzzards Bay into the Herring River. Bourne was part of Sandwich, and present-day Bournedale was the village of North Sandwich.

The Bournedale herring run eventually terminates in Great and Little Herring Ponds, large spawning ponds about a mile to the north, but I was curious where the fish went in between. Less than a quarter-mile north of the canal on Bournedale Road I came to the Carter-Beal Conservation Area, a 31-acre property acquired by the town in 1977. The area includes a small park bracketed by the Herring River, which splits into two streams at this point. On the west side a wide and rather slow-flowing stream empties out of a small millpond, down another series of older, small fish ladders, and under the road. This was full of fish heading upstream. On the east side are the ruins of an old brick mill flume through which the water drops six feet from the millpond above. Herring were also massed here, but they had no way to get up into the pond above the flume.

Fronting the road is a low, belichened stone wall with a stone pillar entrance that looked like it might have been the driveway to some now-vanished estate. But the most unexpected find of all was a wooden sign inscribed, "Maintained by CC HOG in memory of fallen members," and near it a large granite boulder engraved rather elegantly with a representation of two motorcycle pistons and the legend: "Cape Cod Harley Owners' Group — Pocasset Mass. — Dedicated to all our fallen brothers and sisters, May 1999."

Well, this beat even the swimming pool. Fortunately, just then, a Bournedale natural resources officer pulled in in his truck. His name was Charles Merritt, and he kindly provided some answers to the many questions that had been piling up in my mind.

"That's right," he said. "Every year the Cape Cod HOGs have a Blessing of the Bikes hereabouts, and the Bournedale members come up here with their children. See, there's a heart they made out of wire with spruce branches woven through it. They spend a lot of time keeping up the area, mowing the lawn, taking care of the planted gardens, and so on."

Then he explained to me that the old mill flume had once been an axe factory. "It's a complicated system here. The run does split here, below the road. The wider stream was intended to be the main run, with ladders built for the fish. But herring are a sensory-oriented fish, attracted to the sound of falling water, and unfortunately a lot of them get misdirected over to the mill flume. They're more or less trapped there — they can't get up that flume."

"So what happens to those fish?" I asked. "Do they eventually figure it out and go up the other way?"

"Some of them do, but the majority don't. Some die, and some of them just spawn there."

"I thought alewives had to spawn in calm water."

"Not necessarily. There are some eddies down there, right by the edge of the road, that are pretty still, and they manage. Some years ago the Commonwealth installed a couple of large PVC pipes with flaps on them at the entrance to the main stream. The idea was that the flapping would make noise like falling water and attract more fish that way and, well, it worked and it didn't work."

"Why don't they just put a screen or some other kind of gate at the flume entrance?"

"They tried that, but debris clogs up the screen and then the private property bordering the stream gets flooded."

"So they're just artificially concentrated over there because they can't go anywhere."

"That's right — although it makes a prime spot for poaching!"

I asked him about the motel swimming pool. "Well, when they built Route 6, they did all that work down by the motel, putting in the pool and ladders on the property there. The state has a fish counter down there, just above the pool. It's a piece of 10- or 12-inch PVC pipe with electrodes in it, and every time a fish passes through he hits one of those electrodes and he's counted."

"Did the town of Bourne ever sell the rights to the herring to private commercial firms the way other Cape towns like Brewster did?"

"No, I'll tell you what we had here. When I first came on the job some fifteen years ago we had a recreational fishery down there by the motel. Anyone could show up with a permit and get a trashcan full of herring. Commercial fishermen, with a $75 permit, they could back a pickup truck to the pool and just load it up using a seine, for bait, you know. Well, then they came to find out that the fish were in bad shape — too much gill netting offshore, and Russian, Canadian, and other foreign fleets depleting the stocks, so they closed the run to taking."

"So residents aren't allowed to take any fish now?"

"No, the only way you get herring now is with a $25 permit. We have what you'd call a catching service that's run by town employees. Right now it's three days a week during the spring season. You produce the permit and they get you 15 to 20 fish a day out of the catching pool."

"Oh, so you don't actually get to catch the fish yourself — someone catches them for you."

"Well, the only way you can get them yourself is if the catching service is closed and there's no one there. Now, you can go down to the Canal outside the buffer zone, which runs about 150 feet east and

DIRECTIONS

From the Sagamore
Bridge rotary, go
about 1 mile west on
Route 6 to the Cape
Cod Canal Herring
Run Visitor Center on
your left. The best
viewing of the herring
is in late April or
early May. The
Herring Run Motel is
private property. To
visit the Carter-Beal
Conservation Area,
take a right on
Bournedale Road just
before the Cape Cod
Canal Herring Run
Recreation Area.
Stay left at the fork
onto Herring Pond
Road. Immediately
beyond the fork on
your right is the con-
servation area. Hours
of access during the
spring herring run are
8:00 A.M. to
4:30 P.M. daily.

150 feet west of the run entrance, and there — with a permit, mind you — you can snag your quota of fish by casting."

"It's funny, I've lived on the Cape for many years, I've passed that motel many times, and I never knew there was a park here."

"There's a lot of people live in this town don't know it's here. It's a beautiful property. There used to be a big old house on the stone foundation over there." (I later checked it out. In the 1880 Atlas there is a large house labeled "N. Beals," just west of the "Old Axe Works.")

"Just so you know," he said, "this place closes at 4:30 and we'll be locking the gates — you don't want to get locked in."

I assured him I wouldn't and thanked him for his information. After he left, I walked up a broad trail that follows the river and goes through some lovely little grottoes of young white pines, some old pitch pines, and smaller oaks. Taking a fork to the left, I climbed up a fairly steep trail into the Bournedale Hills, where I passed through a lovely beech forest, a small grove of trees with its young leaves just coming out with the wonderful look of a lime-green fountain, all frozen and trembling in the air. At the crest I found a small abandoned rock quarry with some cut granite sills, perhaps the source of the sills on which the old Carter-Beal mansion was built.

It was time to go. As I retraced my steps back down to the car, I could not help but contemplate what an odd and varied tapestry of elements comprise the Bournedale Herring Run: The original Monument and Herring Rivers have been altered beyond recognition into the very human design of the Cape Cod Canal. The run itself is perhaps the most urbanized and least traditional herring run on the Cape: a series of purely functional concrete culverts and ladders that leads into a motel swimming pool, and from there conducts the fish through a PVC pipe where they are electronically counted. When they reach the conservation area another plastic pipe tries to lure them in the right direction, and the whole place is cared for by volunteers from a motorcycle club.

Not exactly a scene from Patti Page's "Old Cape Cod" — and yet, the fish don't seem to mind. I couldn't help but envy the tourists that used to share the pool with the herring, especially in late summer when the tiny inch-long herring fry were making their way back down the run to the ocean, where they would mature for three or four years before returning to their native ponds to spawn the next generation. Did the swimmers even notice them? And if they did, did they recognize the ancient and enduring ritual of human use and natural renewal of which they were a part?

On the Shoulders of a Giant.

IN A BOOK TITLED *CAPE COD AND THE OFFSHORE Islands*, Walter Teller wrote the following paean to the virtues of the then recently completed Mid-Cape Highway:

—*If Cape Cod's old roads are beautiful, the new, in their way, are more so. Broad and unspoiled, they slice through where no trail existed before. They show remarkable morainal profiles; they reveal grand ice-molded contours. They pass through terrain you could hardly otherwise see. . . . The more I traveled the great Mid-Cape U.S. 6 Highway, the more commanding I found it. Limited access, generous right of way. Wide, open-armed, running high or cutting deep, this uncluttered new route unveils panoramas and sparsely settled pine-covered miles. . . .*

Few writers since have had the temerity to apply the term "great" to Cape Cod's major highway, or any highway for that matter; but I have always admired Teller for his recognition that this artery did afford a new experience of the glacial hills of the Upper Cape. When the Mid-Cape Highway was first completed in the late 1950s, drivers along the stretch from Sandwich to West Barnstable did indeed experience the feeling of traveling through a virtually unbroken forested wilderness. It was the first glimpse that most travelers had had of one of the Cape's more remote areas: the high wooded hills of the Sandwich moraine. This moraine was created some 20,000 years ago when the last ice sheet to cover the Cape paused in its retreat, depositing enormous ridges of sand, clay and rock at its edge. Until recently this area remained sparsely settled, with few paved roads through it.

In the last decade or so Teller's "uncluttered new route" has become increasing cluttered and the view more and more broken with new subdivisions, golf courses, schools and other signs of our spreading occupation of this land. Ironically, it was the creation of the Mid-Cape Highway (or, more accurately, the "service roads" that were built parallel to it) that finally provided easy access to these once-isolated areas, and brought with it the accelerating development that had hit most other parts of the Cape earlier.

Fortunately, the town of Sandwich recognized the unique and valuable character of the moraine ecosystem and over several decades has acquired a number of parcels on either side of the Mid-Cape Highway as open space. The largest of these is the Maple Swamp Conservation Area, a 500-acre expanse of woodland straddling the spine of the Cape, which, although it encompasses some of the loftiest terrain on the entire peninsula, is somewhat incongruously named for one of its lowest features: an extensive maple swamp that sits in a large kettle hole in the center of the property.

Though there are some higher points elsewhere on the Cape, there is no place where the landscape swoops, dips and rises on such a dramatic scale. Right away one senses that the geography has an unusual heft and expanse to it. The hills rise up in succeeding levels that are more reminiscent of the Berkshire foothills than of the sandy Cape. There are abundant large glacial boulders scattered about, and the old wood roads are paved with stones and small flat rocks, so that one is tempted to think there is actual bedrock

underneath, rather than several hundred feet of stratified glacial drift. The mind knows it is an illusion, of course, but the feet are convinced otherwise.

The woods are nearly solid oak, interspersed with small stands of beech and red maples in the swamps. The oaks have recovered from the devastation of the last century when they were completely stripped from these hills to feed the furnaces of the nearby Sandwich Glass Works. (Ironically, this famous industry did not use local sand, which was abundant but too impure; instead, sand was imported from New Jersey!) But there are also a number of unusually large white pines towering above the oaks, monarchs that were perhaps spared because they did not burn as hotly as oak.

Every season in a place has its own pleasures. I first visited here on a cool day in early June, at the peak of the year's new green foliage. The just-unfolded oak leaves, still largely untouched by chewing insects, seem to glow with inner verdant vitality. The banks of the wood roads were lined with the dark green leathery leaves of the trailing arbutus, or mayflower. Mayflowers, I have noticed, are always most abundant in this microhabitat. The coming of wood roads must have greatly increased the prevalence of our state flower. I was a month too late for its diminutive, sweet-smelling flowers, but the voluptuous, graceful blossoms of lady's slippers, those lovely woodland orchids, were strewn among the woods, framed artistically against the maidenhair fern that grows here. There are places where lady's slippers grow in spectacular gatherings of several hundred, but I find that I prefer them like this, spaced infrequently along the trail. They seem more companionable that way. They seem to greet you, almost to expect you. In other places I spotted the sweet diminutive pink clusters of sheep laurel. In Newfoundland this wildflower is known as "goo-witty," a name I have always thought more expressive of the little pink-candy appearance of the blossoms, which look as if they were molded out of pink sugar.

I began climbing toward one of the "scenic overlooks," marked "S" on the map. (These are more strenuous trails than are found on most Cape walks and are not to be undertaken lightly on hot and humid summer days.) A beautiful mourning cloak butterfly floated beside me for several yards, and in another place a gleaming, emerald-gold beetle lay like a small jewel in my path. The woods were fairly quiet for mid-June, except for cries of a catbird, the "teacher-

teacher" calls of an ovenbird, and a hairy woodpecker *tat-tat-tatting* on some dead pine snag.

That is, I assumed it was a hairy because that is the woodpecker I expect to hear in Cape Cod woodlands. But when I looked at it on the snag I realized that it was actually a pileated woodpecker, a large bird with a spectacular red crest, a rare nester on the Cape, and seldom seen much further down-Cape. But these large pine snags in such secluded woodlands provide the kind of nesting habitat this bird requires. It took off, spreading its spectacular black and white wings and uttering its charismatic lunatic laugh as it flew away, as if to say, "You bet these are big woods, buddy!"

With the morning sun slanting through the tall pillars of the trunks of oak and pine, these woods reminded me of that wonderful passage in Thoreau's "Walking" in which he saunters through similar woods and envisions

Some ancient and altogether admirable and shining family [that] had settled there . . . to whom the sun was servant, who had not gone into society in the village. . . . The pines furnished them with gables as they grew. Their house was not obvious to vision; the trees grew through it. I do not know whether I heard the sounds of suppressed hilarity or not. They seemed to recline on the sunbeams. They have sons and daughters. They are quite well.

Then all at once the woods exploded in front of me: a reddish-brown blur tumbled across my line of sight, crash-landing on the other side of the road, followed by a series of small mini-explosions behind it, then a series of high whistles. My heart stopped, and it took me several seconds to put this chaos together. The large explosion was a female ruffed grouse, now squawking and performing her broken-wing act a few yards in front of me. The smaller explosions were her brood of chicks, little brown pinches of fluff that had jumped off to the left and now quickly became immobile and invisible in the underbrush. I remained still, and in a minute or so the mother quieted down, uttering a little catbird-like call, while the little fluffs remained hidden and quiet among the huckleberries.

When I finally reached the overlook summit, I found a small cleared oak grove equipped with a new picnic table. A swath of trees had been cut to the north, providing an impressive view across the Scorton Creek marshes to the clotted line of beach houses on Scorton Neck and the blue waters of Cape Cod Bay beyond. The elevation here is nearly 250 feet, not quite one-twentieth of a mile. This is not very impressive by mainland standards, but it gave me a sense of giddiness nonetheless. The contours of the land seemed to drop away endlessly into vast green cauldrons or bowls into which the mind could sink, fall apart, and bathe luxuriously in the non-human variousness of it all, before reassembling itself, refreshed. (But, as if to keep me honest, I could also see, far and away at the ridges of the horizon, the swooping arcs of the Cape's main power lines carrying our necessary river of electricity all the way out to Provincetown.)

On that morning these burly morainal hills suggested the shoulders of Maushop, the benevolent giant of Wampanoag lore. Many of the local Indian creation myths seem to acknowledge the correspondence of the Cape's landscape with the human body. In these tales landforms are either created by the actions of figures like Maushop, or are themselves human beings transformed, by magic or by the gods, into parts of the Cape itself. Science is, of course, essential to understanding our world, but there are times (and this was one of them) when for all my acquired knowledge of the geological and ecological history of places like this, the old Wampanoag creation stories seem to go more directly to the heart of its nature.

In addition to the main trails shown on the town guide, there are a number of small, unmarked side paths that invite you to explore them. One I took led down to a little maple-shaded swamp that was ringed with deer, raccoon, and other animal tracks. At dawn or dusk this place must be a festival of birdsong. Large swamp maples spread their flat canopies out over the water, which was filled with wriggling polliwogs, fulfilling its biological function as a vernal pool.

———————

It is impossible to describe all the features of an area as large and varied as this one in a short essay, and even if I could it would be misleading. It is not my intention to write about generic land-scapes, as if a place like this were something less than itself, or more than itself, some "representative" landscape, an exemplar, or template (e.g., "an oak-pine recessional moraine") — as if it could be captured in one verbal snapshot, or even abstracted.

DIRECTIONS

Take Exit 3 off the Mid-Cape Highway (Quaker Meeting-house Road). Immediately south of the highway, turn left onto the Service Road and follow it east 1.1 miles. The sign and parking lot for the Maple Swamp Conservation Area are on your right.

Each special place is not only individual and unique, but exists only in its own present, on a day-to-day basis, and that is how it has to be discovered. I sometimes think of these essays not as guides so much as invitations. I can, for instance, tell you a few stories about a place like this, enough, I hope, to prompt you to come see it for yourself. But if you do, you will not see the same woods I saw. The woods I experienced in early June, for example, are not the same ones you will encounter if you go out on a winter's day. The green leafy labyrinth of summer will have fallen away, and instead there will stand endless aisles of gray pillars, with crabbed brown leaves rattling on the twigs. The wildflowers will be long gone, and in their place there will be the sweet, red berries of the wintergreen for you to taste, and the large fallen cones of the white pine for you to gather for decorating holiday wreathes. The butterflies and beetles will have vanished, and the grouse broods grown up and dispersed, but through the bare oak branches you may spot the warm flanks of a red-tailed hawk sailing over the maple swamp or catch the white flash of a deer's tail as its ebony hooves drum along the frozen ground.

Even if you visit on the same day of the year as I did, you will see a different place. You will not see that butterfly, that woodpecker, that shining emerald beetle, that frantic grouse; and even if you did, your own perceptions, expectations, and readiness to see certain things and ignore others would make it a different experience. All that is certain, barring another ice age, is that you will encounter these magnificent, morainal hills, whose folded contours, in the words of Cape folklorist Elizabeth Reynard, "explain themselves, as if a spirit-being looked upon them with wisdom."

A map of Sandwich's conservation and recreation land is available from the Conservation Department (508-888-4200), but the trail guides are suggestive rather than detailed, and it is easy to get lost. This is not necessarily a bad thing, but you should be prepared if you are not willing to be lost. Especially on cloudy days, it is advisable to bring a compass and a topographical map of the area.

Mashpee
JOHN'S POND PARK

An Uncertain Harvest.

IN JULY AND AUGUST, THE TOWN BEACH AT THE
north end of John's Pond is by far the most popular freshwater
swimming beach in Mashpee. The parking lot is packed and hundreds of bodies line the 1200 feet of sandy shoreline at the north
end of this 317-acre great pond (one of the Cape's largest). The picnic tables on the adjacent rise of upland provide spectacular vistas of
the pond and the surrounding wooded shoreline, and there is a new
playground for kids beside the parking lot. Most of the people here
are local families, for the beach is not easy to find if you do not
know where it is.

During the summer, held by the magnet of the beach and the pond's clear blue waters, relatively few visitors are tempted to explore the woodlands to the east. But those who do will find one of the Cape's hidden conservation gems, acquired by the town with state Self-Help funds in 1983 and 1984. Few town conservation areas contain the variety of freshwater and forest habitats that are incorporated in Mashpee's 233-acre John's Pond Park.

On the shoreline just east of the public beach is an old dam and wooden fish ladder. Here the pond waters empty into the head-waters of the Quashnet River Valley, a five-mile long river corridor that eventually empties into Waquoit Bay. John's Pond is unusual in that it is the source of two rivers, the Quashnet and Child's River, both of which are part of the Waquoit Bay watershed. Only the link with Child's River is natural, however. One hundred and fifty years ago the citizens of Mashpee decided to dig a connection between the headwaters of the Quashnet River and John's Pond in order to provide water to the commercial cranberry bogs downstream and to increase the Quashnet's alewife or migratory herring population by giving the fish access to the spawning areas in the pond. The ditch flows into a small cedar swamp — the original source of the river — then through a cattail swamp, and then into a large working cran-berry bog, which in the past has been leased out by the town to commercial growers.

Just to the north of the town beach is Moody Pond, a smaller body of water that flows into John's Pond. Even in midsummer, the quiet and relatively unvisited shores of Moody Pond provide solitude and respite from the crowds. Mallards, black ducks, colorful wood ducks and other waterfowl frequent its shallow waters and wooded shores, and a small wooded island in the center tempts the kayaker and canoeist from the landing on its south end.

It is in the fall, however, that both of these ponds and the park's other wetlands and woodlands come into their own. Just east of the beach at John's Pond is a grove of large tupelo trees, or black gum. These water-loving trees provide some of our most resplendent early autumn foliage. Their small ovate leaves turn bright scarlet and gold, contrasting with the dark-blue berries on the female trees, which provide forage for large flocks of starlings. Standing beneath the tupelos in late September is like standing beneath a stained glass ceiling that is slowly collapsing into soft shards.

At Moody Pond, a footpath winds north along the western shore for several hundred feet, ending in a grove of tall, slim white pines 60 to 70 feet high. Swamp maples line the shore here, and in early October their foliage turns gold, yellow-green, orange-red, and deep purple-red. Many of the leaves fall into the pond and form floating Persian carpets of multihued patterns. But the leaves also fall along the paths, and a little later in the season, when the white pines selectively shed their needles, they fall across the brighter maple leaves like a light tan veil over a brilliantly colored mosaic.

Nearly four miles of dirt roads and maintained trails connect the park's various wetland habitats, cranberry bogs, swamps, marshes, old sand pits, and mature second-growth forests of pitch pine, mixed oak, stately white pine, dense stands of beech, fragrant sassafras groves, and some of the largest hollies on the Upper Cape. It is in such forests that I realize again what an unhomogeneous place the Cape is. On the Outer Cape, where I live, several of these species — like beech, white pine and holly — are unusual. On the other hand, plant species like bearberry and broom crowberry, which are abundant in places in Wellfleet and Truro, are uncommon on the Upper Cape.

The extensive cranberry bogs at the eastern end of the park provide their own seasonal parade of visual delights. In spring the newly greened vines are dotted with thousands of small, white, nodding blossoms in the shape of miniature crane heads — said to have given the "crane-berry" its name. Since the main stream of the Quashnet flows directly through these bogs, it is possible to watch herring swimming upstream through the bog ditches towards John's Pond in April and May, flanked by crowds of white blossoms. In summer the bogs are sunken lakes of intense green, the small, hard unripe berries blending in among the vines. By mid-September the thumbnail-sized berries have begun to ripen into their harvest colors, ranging from pink to deep red; and later still, after the harvest, the vines themselves turn their wine-dark winter hue before they are flooded to protect their roots from freezing.

There is, however, a cloud over these bogs. When I visited the bogs in September, after the commercial cranberry harvest was over, the thick crop of ripe cranberries remained unpicked. Since 1995, in fact, the crops of the Quashnet bogs have been deliberately destroyed. They are forbidden fruit, tainted by small amounts of a known carcinogen — ethyl-dibromide — better known as EDB. Less than a half-mile north of these bogs lies Otis Air Force Base, part of the massive 15,000-acre Massachusetts Military Reservation. EDB is an additive in jet fuel, and over the past decade it has shown up in several underground water plumes on the Upper Cape, seeping into ponds, bogs, rivers, and town aquifers.

The Massachusetts Military Reservation is, as most Cape Codders are all too aware, a federally designated Superfund Site — that is, it is a major source of toxic pollutants that threaten the municipal water supplies of several Upper Cape towns. The Pentagon has already spent years and millions of dollars developing plans and techniques to avoid or minimize contamination of drinking water supplies by these plumes — with still uncertain results.

Here in John's Pond Park, a number of metal well pipes have been installed along the northern border to monitor groundwater feeding the ponds and the bogs. Although the amounts of measured contamination found in these berries have been small, the state Environmental Protection Agency has developed a zero-tolerance policy for EDB, so that, as long as any contamination is found, the crops must be destroyed. A series of dikes has been constructed around the bogs in an attempt to halt the movement of contaminated groundwater into the bogs, but as this book goes to press the prognosis for having a saleable crop this year is not good.

So once again the links between human and natural systems have proven peculiarly knotty and complex because of the interconnected nature of the Cape's underground aquifer. The contamination of the Quashnet bogs is particularly worrisome given their direct connections to Waquoit Bay, which is already under stress from septic runoff and other chemical and organic pollutants. Moreover, John's Pond Park is part of the ambitious Mashpee National Wildlife Refuge, a 5,871-acre preserve established in 1995 within the Waquoit Bay watershed, a landmark venture involving the cooperation and ownership of various federal, state, town, private, and tribal organizations. What should be the jewel of the Upper Cape's open spaces contains a flaw that threatens the integrity of the entire system.

I visited the park again in late October after several days of heavy rains. The beach and parking lot at the pond were deserted. Stiff westerly gusts kicked up dark waves along the shore, and only a few

DIRECTIONS

Finding John's Pond can be confusing for the first-time visitor. From the rotary on Route 28 in Mashpee, take Route 151 west 2.5 miles. Just past the Mashpee–Sandwich town line, turn right on Ashumet Road at the turnoff for the Massachusetts Audubon Society Ashumet Holly and Wildlife Sanctuary. At the intersection with Hooppole Road, turn right and go another 1.8 miles to a stop sign at Back Road. Turn right and go 0.5 mile down to the town beach. *Note:* Mashpee beach stickers are required during the summer.

ring-billed gulls played in the wind. The once brilliant tupelos had been stripped of their autumn glory, and only a few leaves still hung on the stiff black branches. When I came to the bogs I found that they were partially flooded by the rains. The main stream of the Quashnet River and the side ditches had become broad watery highways, on which several small flocks of mallards and black ducks were floating and feeding. I could not help but wonder what effect, if any, the invisible pollutants in the bogs might have on such aquatic wildlife over time. As I watched the ducks through my binoculars, they suddenly flew up and scattered as a broad shadow, like a giant black palm, spread across them. I looked up, and, with a noise like chopping thunder, the dark form of a military helicopter rose above the ridge of pines beyond the bogs.

A Place out of Time.

THERE ARE MANY TOWNS ON THE CAPE THAT HAVE
more conservation land than Mashpee does, yet Mashpee has what
almost no other town does: an extensive greenbelt running right
through the middle of its town center. It begins at a town park at the
headwaters of the Mashpee River on Mashpee Pond and follows the
river south through the village along an "emerald necklace" of town-,
state-, and land trust-owned parcels.

Moreover, this central greenbelt is part of a nearly continuous corridor of open space running the entire length of Mashpee, from the
justly famous Lowell Holly Reservation that juts between Wakeby and

Mashpee Ponds, to the river-bordering uplands of the Mashpee River Woodlands running into Popponesset Bay, to the Mashpee National Wildlife Refuge and South Cape Beach State Park on Vineyard Sound.

Of all this magnificent network of green space, the largest of the central village properties, the Mashpee River Reservation, is also the least known. The 248-acre property is owned by The Trustees Of Reservations, the oldest private land trust in the world. Established in 1891 by Charles Eliot of Boston, The Trustees Of Reservations (TTOR) is custodian of over 17,500 acres of conservation land in the Commonwealth. The bulk of the Mashpee River Reservation was acquired by a gift in 1959. It begins just south of the village center, encompassing most of the land on both sides of the river between Great Neck and Meetinghouse Roads. Parking and access are from a series of town-owned properties off Meetinghouse Road.

Unlike the more developed Mashpee River Woodlands south of Route 28, the Mashpee River Reservation has no established trail system or map, so that exploring it is something of an adventure. For those not familiar with the terrain, I would suggest a winter or early spring excursion, when the woods are leafless and it is easier to orient oneself.

The easiest public access is the town-owned Fitch property, located on the west side of Meetinghouse Road about a mile south of the town center. From the new gravel parking lot there are two informal trails heading into the woods. The one on the left is broader and goes south through to Asher's Path, where there is access to the river. The one on the right heads due west, but peters out after a while. However, in late April, when I visited the reservation, the oak leaves were still furled and the woods had an open feel to them, so I decided to take the trail on the right and head directly for the river.

The woods are mostly mixed oak and pitch pine, with scattered holly and beech. But the land also contains some of the most majestic specimens of white pine anywhere on the Cape, many of them soaring a hundred feet or more above the ground. Some are "candelabra" pines: tall white pines that split into two and three trunks just a couple of feet above the base and then spire upwards like enormous black tapers. There was one wrecked pine trunk, snapped off about ten feet above the ground, that was well over three feet across, and others broken off about halfway up, but still

alive. There is something about a forest with plenty of large wrecks in it that adds to a sense of primevalness, of something unmanaged and untidied and therefore capable of surprises.

At one point a sudden flash of warm brown haunches and the white flag of a deer materialized and went crashing off into the maze of tree trunks and branches. It seemed much larger than the local deer I am familiar with. In another place the explosive whirring of a ruffed grouse spiraled away from me from the base of a huge pine.

When the trail petered out, I headed west through open woods, occasionally bushwhacking through heavy undergrowth, knowing I would eventually intersect with the river. I heard it before I saw it, for at this point the Mashpee River flows at the bottom of a deep cut in this wooded plateau. When I came to the crest of the cut I could see the water gleaming like a silver thread about 40 feet below. It was a striking sight, for there are few places on the Cape where one can walk through unbroken woods and come to a view of a running river glistening its way down through an undisturbed valley. At the same time I was aware of traffic, slightly elevated above me, on Great Neck Road across the other side of the valley. It was a strange sight, in the middle of this wilderness, as if one or the other were not quite real.

I hoped I might find a continuous path running beside the river, but there was none. Instead, I found myself going up and down the steep bank, occasionally finding definite trails, only to have them peter out again. I continued with some trepidation, for much of the west bank of the river is still privately owned, and at times there was no way to tell if I was on official reservation land or not. Although I tried to avoid obvious house lots, it is one of the characteristics of exploring such "undeveloped" conservation areas that these distinctions between "private" and "public" seemed to grow more blurred and irrelevant as I progressed.

There is a story about the lack of trails on this property that I heard from a local woman whose acquaintance I had made a few years ago. She was a member of the Mashpee Wampanoag tribe, whose ancestors had used the river and its woodlands as hunting and fishing grounds and who regarded them as sacred ground for ritual prayers and offerings. About a decade ago, The Trustees Of Reservations and the Mashpee River Woodlands Association held a public meeting on a proposed trail system running the length of the river corridor. The woman spoke against the proposed trails, warning that there were "beings," or spiritual presences, residing along the river "who might not like the intrusion." A few weeks later there was a fire of mysterious origin along the river. Putting it out required brushbreakers and other heavy equipment. A good part of the woodlands was torn up and portions of the river became heavily silted. The organizations abandoned plans for a trail system, although Jim Freeborn, manager of the Trustees' properties on the Cape and South Shore, told me they hope to construct a trail system "some day."

Despite the lack of clearly marked, continuous trails, I was struck by the numerous signs of use I encountered in this semitrackless semiwilderness. In one place I found a crude table made from a sheet of plywood set up on sawhorses, with a rusty folding chair beside it. In other places there were stools or overturned milk cartons placed out in the middle of the woods for no apparent reason, or more folding chairs placed right along the river, where a number of scallop shells had been thrown in the water.

At one point I happened upon a more complex and mysterious site. It was a holly grove, with about a half dozen large trees forming a shaded clearing right beside the river. Within the clearing were old chairs, tables made out of milk cartons and boards tacked together, and a small campfire. It might have been just an informal campsite made by local kids, but it was remarkably clean and litter-free, as if it were used regularly and maintained.

Although I found no continuous path along the river here, I did come upon a footbridge that looked as if it had been there for some time. It was composed of two horizontal poles with some two-by-six planks nailed at two-foot intervals across them. Crossing it, I could see the wonderful clear bottom of this stream, pure sand with scattered gravel, though there was as yet no sign of herring.

But none of these signs of informal (and no doubt unauthorized) use prepared me for what I stumbled upon deep in the wooded valley, out of sight and sound of all traffic and other signs of our collective modern life. I was making my way along the west bank of the river, and, just where it bent to the east, there were several pine trunks that had been placed across the stream. On the other side was what I can only describe as a small wetu — a traditional dome-shaped Wampanoag dwelling. It was about eight feet in diameter,

DIRECTIONS

From Route 130 in Mashpee center, head south on Great Neck Road for 0.1 mile. Bear left onto Meetinghouse Road for approximately 0.8 mile. From Route 28, take Meetinghouse Road north for 1.0 mile. Look for the Fitch Property sign on the west side of the road, marking the entrance to the gravel parking lot. The path on the left going up the hill will take you south through the reservation to Asher's Path, where there is access to the river. For any other exploration of the property, a compass and a topographical map (US Geological Survey — Cotuit Quadrangle) of the property are recommended.

constructed of four intersecting hoops of arrowwood stems, with smaller hoops on three of the four sides, all connected by strips of bark where they intersected. The hoop structure was covered with a triple layer of canvas. There was a fire pit in the center, and an old, large rack of deer antlers on one side.

On the ground outside were a variety of objects that seemed to indicate recent occupation: a gourd, a cup made out of an old coconut husk, a handmade straw broom with a braided handle and a rounded stone, some small painted pieces of pottery, and some freshly split wood.

The site had a tidy simplicity to it that indicated something other than a casual or ephemeral use. Except for the canvas tarp, this was a scene one might have found here hundreds of years ago. Only a thin trail, not more than a deer trail, really, led to this spot. What is this place? I wondered. More importantly, when is it? I recalled another thing the Wampanoag woman had told me: "The whites have basically three dimensions, maybe four. We have twelve, and even the nearest ones, the ones that take a physical form, may have purposes of their own that lie in the future, or in the past."

Whatever this place was, whenever it was, I knew it was not mine to intrude on; and so I withdrew, eventually rejoining the main trail south and emerging at Asher Path. Later in the season, I revisited the property, hoping to find the mysterious encampment again. But, of course, there was no sign of it.

Heavenly Length.

FELIX MENDELSSOHN, PRAISING FRANZ SCHUBERT'S

Great C Major Symphony, once referred to its "heavenly length." It

is a phrase that comes to mind whenever I behold the unending lines

of wavelike dunes breaking down the long, sandy spine of

Barnstable's Sandy Neck.

Over six miles long and by far the largest of all town-owned open

spaces on Cape Cod, the Sandy Neck ecosystem contains many

worlds. In addition to its impressive dune fields, it includes one of

the most popular bathing beaches on Cape Cod Bay, freshwater

swales and wild cranberry bogs, over 300 species of birds and 85

species of wildflowers, nesting areas for several endangered species,

hidden maritime forests, the largest salt marsh system on the

Northeast coast, a sizeable deer herd, a remote private cottage colony, some of the best bluefish and bass fishing on the Cape, and — perhaps rarest of all — the ability to provide solitude and unexpected encounters at all times of the year.

To most summer visitors, however, Sandy Neck often appears as little more than a packed parking lot and a seemingly unbroken column of ORVs stretching down its outer beach. But to those willing to get off the beaten track and explore a little, the Neck offers up its lesser known secret places. One of these, one of its innermost worlds, is the Marsh Trail.

At the Sandy Neck ranger station, a half-mile before the beach parking lot, head east on foot on the old sand road that runs along the inner edge of the marsh. This road is closed to public traffic, and most times of the year you will have it all to yourself. One day I walked out here on Memorial Day weekend, when thousands of people were at the beach and hundreds of vehicles lined the bay shore. Not another soul made it to the back shore.

But it is more than solitude you will find here. On your left are the beginnings of the Neck's vast dune field, which Timothy Dwight, an early nineteenth-century traveler, described as a "wild and fantastical beach, thrown into a thousand grotesque forms by the actions of wind and waves." To your right is the beginning of the seemingly endless salt prairies of Barnstable's Great Marshes, a 5,000-acre labyrinth of spartina grasses, winding tidal creeks and peat islands — the largest salt marsh system in the Northeast.

Out on the marsh, bordering the road, are dozens and dozens of tree swallow boxes, where in summer these birds breed and raise their young. In June the air is full of their swooping, arcing forms, like bits of winged emeralds, as they sing, warble and feast on thousands and thousands of salt marsh mosquitoes and midges throughout the day. Just as the nesting terns and piping plovers on the outside bay shore are vulnerable to June storms that may sweep their nests off the beaches, so these companionable swallows and their young broods sometimes starve to death when long periods of cold damp weather keep insects out of the air. At such times I have found their nesting box entrances stuffed with grass that the birds have placed there in an apparent attempt to keep out the cold winds.

Though of unusual extent, the dunes and salt marsh are elements found on most barrier beaches. After a mile or so, however, you will enter a world of strange and startling juxtapositions. Now the sandy slopes of the dunes begin to alternate with heavily wooded groves of thick oak, ancient holly, red maple, wild cherry, juniper, and flowering dogwood. These are the maritime forests of Sandy Neck, the product of its unusual geological history.

Barrier beaches are highly dynamic systems; most of them literally roll over on themselves in the face of beach erosion, retreating slowly, year after year. (This is why you will often find large chunks and ledges of marsh peat on the outside beaches of barrier spits, indicating the former site of salt marshes that were once protected behind the beach.) Sandy Neck, almost alone among the Cape's major barrier beach systems, is largely a nonretreating beach. For reasons still not fully understood, it has grown eastward in length over the past 6,000 years or so, but has maintained a stable position relative to the marsh behind it. This unusual stability has allowed for the development of sizeable maritime hardwood forests on its inner edges. If you look at a USGS topographical map of the Neck, these forests are indicated by patches of green of varying size along its length.

Though surrounded, and sometimes buried, by sand dunes, these woods have a strikingly secluded and inland feel to them. Some of the oaks are quite old and large, two feet thick or more. Yet turn a bend in the road and you will see vistas a thousand miles apart: columbine, jack-in-the-pulpit, trout lily, trillium, and other spring wildflowers associated more with rich, inland woods bloom in shaded groves a few yards from marsh saltwort, showy beach rose blossoms, and greening poverty grass ablaze with their tiny, bright yellow June blossoms. Listen and you will simultaneously hear bird-song from very different worlds: yellowthroats and yellowlegs, vireos and willets, flickers and terns, curlews and cardinals, mergansers and mourning doves, sandpipers and song sparrows, marsh hawks and ring-neck pheasants, kingbirds and kingfishers. Squirrels chitter in the overhanging branches of oaks that shade horseshoe crabs sliding along the tide-flooded tracks of beach buggies. Here, if a squirrel fell, it could land on the back of a crab.

The marsh road is also a critical transition zone, or ecotone, in the breeding cycle of Sandy Neck's most celebrated and endangered wild resident: the diamondback terrapin. This large and beautiful marsh turtle is the color of gray and brown sea stones, with powerful webbed claws and a Moorish richness of geometry sculpted across its carapace. A century ago it was prized as a gourmet item, the prime ingredient of terrapin soup. Up to 10,000 diamondbacks a week were once shipped out of Barnstable's Great Marshes to fine restaurants in Boston, New York, and other cities.

As a result, only a remnant of the original population survives today. But it is a significant remnant, for it represents the northernmost breeding population of this species. As such, it has been the subject of one of the longest continuous field studies on the East Coast. For over a quarter century, Dr. Peter Auger, an ecology teacher at Barnstable High School, has monitored, tracked, and analyzed the breeding, migration, and gestation of these terrapins with the help of fellow scientists and scores of volunteer researchers. Dr. Auger is in a line of distinguished scientific researchers on Sandy Neck. One of the first was the late Dr. Alfred Redfield, a Barnstable native and later a professor at the Marine Biological Laboratory in Woods Hole, who conducted the first systematic studies of the formation of salt marshes here in the early twentieth century.

Peter Auger's work has added significantly to the understanding of terrapin biology and of the behavior of species at the fringes of their breeding ranges. Moreover, his findings have resulted in specific regulations designed to provide long-term protection to Sandy Neck's diamondbacks. One such regulation was the banning of public traffic from the marsh road, as the road is a critical ecotone during the turtle's breeding cycles.

From June through August you may come upon a characteristic column of double tracks with a center tail line winding through the dunes, as if a miniature web-footed boat were dragging its keel through the sand. These are the tracks of pregnant female terrapins that crawl out of the marsh across the sand road and up into the dunes to lay their clutches of rubbery, reptilian eggs. Several weeks later the eggs hatch and the tiny turtlings unerringly make their way back down the dune slopes and into the marsh, crossing the same sand road as they do. If you should spot these tracks, or the turtle itself, *do not follow them,* for these animals are easily disturbed.

While walking, you are more likely to see the tracks than the diamondbacks themselves. You can, however, explore the marshes of

DIRECTIONS

Sandy Neck Road goes
north off Route 6A
0.2 mile west of the
Barnstable–Sandwich
town line. Follow the
road to the Sandy
Neck ranger station
where, in the off-sea-
son, you may park in
the small lot next to
it. During the summer
months special per-
mits are required to
park here. For a daily
admission fee, you
may drive to the
beach parking lot and
walk 0.5 mile back to
the ranger station.
The marsh trail
begins immediately
east of the station.
Caution: Portions of
the trail regularly
flood at high tides,
especially during the
monthly spring or
moon tides. Check
the tide schedules or
wear boots.

Sandy Neck by canoe, taking one of the dozens of marsh creeks that branch out from Barnstable Harbor. Here, if you are lucky, you may see the terrapins basking in the sun on exposed mud banks, or courting, with four or five smaller males attendant upon a larger female. One day in early June, a few hours past high tide, I paddled with a companion almost a half-mile up the twisting, narrow course of Great Island Creek in a light northeasterly rain. Great submerged shelves of peat glided beneath us, while black walls of peat rose vertically six or seven feet above us. It was like paddling through shallow black canyons. Peat above us, and even more peat below us, to depths of 20, 30 feet, and more — thousands of years of slow organic building up and layering down, the product of life that has just managed to keep its green head above seawater. The slow dripping of the water from the exposed tips of the cord grass roots onto the peat shelves seemed like the dripping of time itself.

Like the turtles, the old road, following the winding edge of the upland, is curiously amphibious in nature. In places it rises over a sandy bulge where a dune has shouldered out onto the marsh; in others it dips to the level of the marsh where, especially at monthly spring tides, the road becomes a shallow, flowing salt river.

Along the marsh road, you will pass a dozen or more private cottages. Some are tucked back into the forested hill behind the road. Others sit up in the barren dunes, naked to the sky, backed by those flat-topped or sharply truncated dune summits, heavily vegetated with beach grass or beach plums that are so characteristic of Sandy Neck. Some sit right out on the road, with wood posts or stone retaining walls holding them above the tidal waters, and a few are tucked out of sight on small wooded islands that sit out on the marsh. At least one, I was told, built nearly a century ago, had been completely buried by a large walking dune known as The Saddle.

These cottages are, for the most part, solitary, strung out at least a hundred yards, and often several hundred yards, apart, with no more than two or three together in any one spot. (In this they contrast with the compact community of two dozen or so private cottages, clustered like sowbugs in a damp corner, at the very tip of the Neck.) At high tide, with the water flowing right in front of them, and wooded knolls behind, separated by sight from one another by bends in the road, they remind me of shacks I have seen on river banks in Maine or Oregon, or little hill cabins in the hollows and foothills of West Virginia, with green fields spread out around them.

Many of these cottages were originally built as hunting cabins, when duck hunters took advantage of the enormous numbers of waterfowl that took shelter in winter in the marshes and Barnstable Harbor. But the human history of Sandy Neck lies much deeper in its shifting sands. Archaeological evidence suggests that precontact Native Americans used the Neck for seasonal fishing and for ceremonial burials. During the seventeenth century the entire Neck was used as a "commons" for pasturing cattle, and for setting up fish houses and "try yards" for rendering whale blubber, a process which required enormous amounts of firewood and no doubt contributed to the destruction of much of the Neck's original forests. Whalebones still occasionally emerge out of the sides of shifting dunes here.

Parts of the Neck remained in commercial use at least into the 1930s. In places one can still see where sections of the marsh abutting the road were cut off from the main marsh with earthen dikes to create cranberry bogs during the Depression. Such "salt bogs," never very productive, were soon abandoned and subsequently grew up to pitch pines, whose stark black skeletons now stand in tidal waters that have breached the dams. During World War II Sandy Neck was used for bombing practice, and pieces of old scrap metal still show up out in the dunes.

It is hard to conceive of now, but in the 1950s a proposal was made to construct a paved highway down the length of Sandy Neck. Fortunately this plan never materialized, and in the 1950s the town of Barnstable began reacquiring its "commons" for the benefit of all its citizens and visitors. Today all but a few dozen acres of upland are owned by the town, under the management of Barnstable Recreation Department. In 1978 the Commonwealth recognized the Neck's unique resources when the Sandy Neck Barrier Beach System — including all of Sandy Neck, Scorton Neck, Barnstable Harbor, and the entire Great Marsh System — was designated as an Area of Critical Environmental Concern, the first on Cape Cod.

One evening in late June I climbed up out of one of the forested hollows bordering the marsh to a bare sand ridge to watch the sun set over the sea of dunes to the west. It threw a diffused, reddish light over the long, undulating sand valley, giving it an underwater look. In the treetops below me yellowthroats, yellow warblers, kingbirds, and redwings were calling everywhere. Dog, deer, and terrapin tracks followed one another up and down the sides of the dunes. I watched a long pale caterpillar with large red eyes making

Trail maps and historical pamphlets are available at the trailhead.

In addition, the Barnstable Conservation Commission's *Hiker's Guide to Town of Barnstable Conservation Lands and Sandy Neck,* a fine packet of maps and trail guides, is available free at the Barnstable town offices in Hyannis.

its way up the dune, stopping every now and then to make little exploratory rootings in the sand, making threaded tracks, like links in a gold necklace, and finally burrowing into the sand at dark.

I stood and looked westward over the tops of this sunken forest of oaks that tossed and thrashed like a green-gray sea, where does were dropping their June fawns unseen in the hollows, invisible voles and squirrels scurried, rustled, and scolded in the leaves, hidden columbines bloomed like dark red anemones, and blackbirds and catbirds leaped about in short parabolas above the tree crowns and dropped back down, like jumping fish.

The sand was swirled in bands of varying browns and tans like fudge ripple. Straggling up the flanks of the bordering forested hills were the broken, blasted, burnt-looking trunks of old beach plum bush-es, now detached, like jettisoned rocket boosters, from the still-living plant that had managed to keep up and reach the top of the 40-foot dune. Long, snaking curves of black sandy loam suggested the interface of long-buried forests with vanished dunes that once arched up into space where wide empty bowls now sink below.

Heavenly length, yes — and unsounded depths as well. Here are worlds within worlds, with new worlds in the making.

Footing It on the Neck.

ONE OF THE THINGS I HAVE ALWAYS LIKED about the names of the land on Cape Cod is how many terms they share with the human body. Thoreau, of course, immortalized the Cape as "the bare and bended arm of Massachusetts," extending the image to include the "fist" at Provincetown, the "elbow or crazy bone" at Chatham, and the "shoulder" at Buzzard's Bay. (Some residents of the Lower Cape mix the metaphor somewhat by referring to the Atlantic shore as the Cape's "backside.")

In addition to this overarching figure, there are such local anatomical appellations as "Money Head" in Orleans, "Hector's Stubble" in Truro, "Back River" in Bourne, "The Gut" in Wellfleet, and "Devil's Foot" in Woods Hole, not to mention more racy placenames such as "Shapely Bottom," "Betty's Curve," "Lucy's Crotch," and "Slut's Bush."

These terms have always suggested to me a kind of instinctive identification with the human scale of the Cape's landscape. But of all of these anatomical names, the one most common by far is "neck" — a term applied to a wide variety of local peninsulas. There are dozens of "necks" on Cape Cod, some in almost every town, but one of the most beautiful is unquestionably Crocker Neck in Cotuit.

Located in the extreme southwest corner of Barnstable, Crocker Neck is a 97-acre town conservation area that is part of a large spreading peninsula projecting into Popponesset Bay. It is one of the true jewels of local open spaces, containing a wealth of habitats, wildlife, and stunning views. Like all true prizes, it is a little difficult to find, but the Barnstable Conservation Commission will provide you, at no charge, with a fine set of maps and trail guides to this and other major town holdings. Visitors may drive through the property along a dirt road known as The Lane all the way to a small beach at its southern tip. On my first visit there, however, I chose to explore it on foot, parking at the north gate trail entrance on Santuit Road.

Usually I avoid trail guides on my initial visit to a new area, not wanting a preconceived set of discoveries. But the guide for Crocker Neck had such a personable and inviting tone that I let it guide my general progress. I set off along the Dike Trail on a beautiful high summer day, the air warm but dry, cool in the shade, with a nice breeze coming off the water. Here one walks along a nice, wide grassy path bordered with thick brushy undergrowth: scrub oak, young maple, and cherries — a young hardwood forest growing up under an aisle of mature pitch pine.

The Dike Trail borders the upper part of Fullers Marsh and gets its name from a dike built in the previous century in order to create a cranberry bog. The thick, pungent odor of sweet pepperbush growing in the low wet borders of the marsh scented the trail, and off to the left I could see where some of the pitch pines had died off,

likely killed by salt water when the bog was abandoned. The old tide gate that kept out the seawater is long gone, and phragmites, or reed grass, has invaded the upper parts of the marsh. A soft breeze was blowing through its tall, dry, feather-topped stems, creating a whispery rattling all around me.

I was in a mood to stand there and just absorb what the place had to say to me, but the place had other ideas. I once wrote a piece about how each season here creates its own perspective and dictates the way we see it. Winter, I wrote, blows us briskly along, forcing us to keep moving, to take in the landscape in sweeps and glances of the eye, large bracing gulpfuls, major outlines only. Summer, on the other hand, I said, invites us to linger, to open our senses and wait patiently for the secrets of the moment to reveal themselves.

I obviously forgot about deerflies. Despite the fact that I was wearing a long-sleeved shirt, a broad-brimmed hat, and had slathered myself in DEET, the deerflies were out in numbers that routed me along as fast as any December gale.

From the Dike Trail one looks south across the marsh to a small island that contains an osprey pole and nest, where a pair of these fish hawks has successfully nested for the past several years. The recovery of ospreys from DDT poisoning in southeastern Massachusetts is one of the great wildlife success stories of the past twenty-five years — so much so, in fact, that in some places, such as Martha's Vineyard, biologists believe the osprey population has reached the saturation point and erection of further poles has been discouraged.

From the Dike Trail I joined the Bank Trail, a path that runs along the top of a steep embankment overlooking the lower marsh. A welcome breeze here helps to keep down deerflies and greenheads in summer. Here I consulted the trail guide, which pointed out several pits that were "probably dug by hunters of marsh ducks years ago," though for what purpose is not clear. But I liked the chatty and proprietary tone of the guide, which refers to the osprey as "our fish hawk" and to "Crocker Neck's great horned owl." It reminded me of Robert Frost's description of his adopted state of New Hampshire as having "One each of everything as in a showcase." There was one sign for a deer run crossing, as if that were the only place that deer ever crossed. In another place, I was invited to "Go ahead and eat a huckleberry," though I was several weeks too early to take advantage of the invitation.

The Bank Trail intersects with Cove Trail, an old wood road that leads down to Pinquickset Cove, an Algonquin Indian name that, as the guide points out, is "a fun name to say." As I walked along this trail I heard a strange but familiar sound, an almost mechanical *whuh-whuh-whuh-whuh-whuh,* like a toy helicopter. I looked up to see the huge, elongated, diaphanous, translucent form of a mute swan ploughing the sky, heading west over the trees towards Shoestring Bay. The mute swan, an imported European species, is a common sight on many of our ponds and estuaries, but many environmentalists do not welcome it, as its aggressive presence tends to discourage native waterfowl from nesting. Yet when it takes off and rows through the air on its powerful eight-foot wingspan, it stirs something profound and primitive in the soul.

Number 7 on the trail map took me off the Cove Trail to a small stand of white pines with a single picnic table in the center. The dense pines formed a little hushed cathedral. The ground, free of any undergrowth, was covered with reddish-brown needles, like a richly woven rug. It was deeply quiet there, a profound silence. Although I knew these pines must have been planted comparatively recently, they seemed very ancient, as if this were a place for sacred rites. Several of the pines are multitrunked and assume grotesque human forms, almost like antique statuary around the altar of the picnic table.

In this place, just as the guide says, the wind makes "a soothing, whishing sound" and "the sun is warm and the falling needles give off a toasty smell." Standing there, I was suddenly transported back several decades to my first summer on Cape Cod, to a place very much like this, on a point of land covered with pines overlooking a saltwater estuary. The summer sun shone on those pines, too, and the smell of warm resin became the smell of Cape Cod to me forever.

I stepped back out into the bright world of sun and space and continued down to Pinquickset Cove. Here, overlooking the blue waters, is an area known as the Pine Grove. It is a classic pine barren: tall, open, widely spaced pitch pines with native grasses and wildflowers growing beneath. Pine barrens and their associated flora are becoming increasingly rare, due to forest succession, development, and fire suppression.

One of the flowers that bloom here in summer is the brilliantly colored butterfly weed, *Asclepias tuberosa.* Here, on this open bluff, the breeze was strong enough to keep down the deer flies and I

DIRECTIONS

From Cotuit center, go west on School Street 0.4 mile and turn left onto Crocker Neck Road. Follow Crocker Neck Road (which turns into Santuit Road) approximately 1.0 mile to the north gate trailhead parking area. Additional parking is just down the road. Look for the Crocker Neck Conservation Area sign on the left. You may drive down the dirt road (The Lane) to a small parking area on the right, or continue another 0.5 mile down to the beach. Trail guides and maps are available from the Barnstable Conservation Commission: 508-790-6245.

stooped to observe this remarkable and maligned "weed." Each of its small, bright, fiery-orange blossoms has five upturned petals ending in hooks, with five larger downturned sepals beneath, creating an elegant sculpted look. A member of the milkweed family, the butterfly weed gets its name from its role as a major food source for monarchs and other lepidoptera. One of its more surprising functions is that of a potential archaeological indicator. Milkweeds prefer a more alkaline soil than the Cape usually provides, and, according to Fred Dunford, staff archaeologist at the Cape Cod Museum of Natural History, their presence may indicate a prehistoric Indian midden of clam shells, whose calcium sweetens the soil enough to allow these plants to flourish.

Once common in New England, the butterfly weed has grown increasingly scarce, and maintaining habitats like this one is crucial to its continued survival, and that of the insect species that feed on it. Stoop to admire it, but practice environmental forbearance and do not pick it.

The Cove Trail connects with the Tide Pool Trail, named for an observation deck with benches overlooking a small tidal pool. The pool is encircled by salt marsh grass and an outer ring of marsh elder bushes, the only local woody plant that can survive in salt water.

One of the remarkable things about Crocker Neck is the constantly changing habitats that it presents. One moves from freshwater marsh to open pines to salt marsh to dense white pine groves to abandoned bogs to shrub swamp, tidal pools, beach, estuarine flats to open water — almost as if passing a series of environmental dioramas. Along the lower part of the Tide Pool Trail the nature of the terrain alters again. The road itself turns to white sand, while the forest changes to mature oak, interspersed with the dead and barkless trunks of their predecessors, the pines. It is as if the place had been landscaped to show off different habitats, as if Frederick Law Olmsted, the great nineteenth-century landscape architect, planned this place as he did Central Park, to look natural. But he didn't, and that's the marvelous thing about it. The rich variety of Crocker Neck is largely just the chance recovery of a variety of native habitats.

Nearly an hour after starting out, I reached the southernmost point of the neck, where the foot trail meets The Lane at a small sandy beach giving onto Popponesset Bay. The beach was crowded, though not with people. It was pocked with hundreds of small holes, into which little fiddler crabs scuttled at my approach. In fact, despite the fact that it was a warm, sunny, summer's day, there was only one other person in sight, a young woman, accompanied by her black lab, who lay sunning herself on a beach chair. She looked utterly languid and peaceful. I said hello and she told me that her boy-friend had just taken the car back to town to get her some bug spray. Chivalry, I thought, is not dead.

The vista south across Popponesset Bay is wide and open. Far to the left across the water is Meadow Point, a wooded headland owned by the Barnstable Land Trust. The thin barrier beach across the horizon is Popponesset Spit, a Mashpee tern-nesting area managed by the Massachusetts Audubon Society. Not only is it a vista of great beauty, but also one of great hope. In 1985 the town of Barnstable bought the 35 acres at the southern end of this property for $3 million to prevent a planned waterfront development from going forward — a price that seems almost cheap now. Yet it is rich testimony that as communities we have learned to cherish and preserve such areas of surpassing natural wealth. It also suggests that, among all of the other anatomical nomenclature we share with the land, we connect with our hearts as well.

Sweet Autumn Mysteries.

WILD GRAPES CAN BE FOUND MOST ANYWHERE ON Cape Cod, but they seem particularly abundant on the North Side from Sandwich to Brewster. Actually, you don't find wild grapes as much as they find you. They usually hit you with their intense, sweet odor before you see them, for they are among the shyest of fruits, hidden beneath their own large, tonguelike leaves and the thick shrubbery they tend to grow among. They are the olfactory counterpart of the spring peepers, whose sound is everywhere, tantalizingly near, but difficult to locate. And when you do find them, they are often hanging from a limb just out of reach, so that you feel like the fox in the old Aesop's fable.

That is the thing about the grapes' smell, too. Their aroma suggests more than their taste could ever equal. It is a lush, plush smell, one of the sweetest and richest bouquets in nature, a smell that promises a beverage, a liquid, far more luscious and inebriating than any actual drink could ever be. The grape jelly I make from them is nice, but it is always something of a disappointment, like beach stones brought home after they dry out. It is on the vine that these wild fruits reach their peak, tantalizing your limbic system with promises of olfactory ecstasy.

It was this seductive fragrance that washed over me like a wave one September morning when I stepped out of my car in the main parking area of Yarmouth's Callery-Darling Conservation Area. Like the wild grapes that are so abundant and hidden along its 2.4 miles of trails, this property tempts the visitor with promises of sweet mystery close by, but just out of view.

Callery-Darling is composed of a rich patchwork of diverse habitats threaded by a trail system that constantly offers the walker alternatives. In fact, one would be hard put to come up with an area of comparable size that has as many different environments and habitats on it as this. There are old cranberry bogs, dikes, old field habitat, thickets, salt marsh, various kinds of woodland, and at least one unexpected botanical rarity.

There is mystery at the very beginning, in fact, for there appear at first to be no trail signs to point the way. If you go to the back of the parking area, however, you will find a large map painted on a piece of plywood covered with a sheet of Plexiglas, showing you three different trail systems. You can, for example, go east across Center Street on a mile-long trail through old fields and cedar groves and along the edge of a salt marsh down to the Gray's Beach picnic area. Or you can go north along a short trail that also takes you to Gray's Beach, where a 1000-foot-long wooden boardwalk stretches out across the salt marsh. In summer the end of the boardwalk is an excellent observation point from which to view the Gray's Beach tern colony, one of the oldest and largest common tern colonies in the state. In recent years an osprey pole has been constructed in the marsh south of the boardwalk, where a pair of these fish hawks raises a brood of chicks each summer. When I last saw it, the nest was about four feet across, still growing, and had as many swatches of plastic sheeting as marsh grass woven into its

mesh, showing that these birds are not proud, or prejudiced, in finding nest material.

You can, for that matter, get a detailed map of the property's trail system from the town's Conservation Department and take it with you; but my suggestion is to study the map in the parking area for a few minutes to get the general lay of the land in your head, and then start off and get benignly lost. That's what I did on that early September morning.

In the fall it is always the western portion of the property that draws me, with its maze of trails, its abundance of fall color, long, dark tunnels of shrubbery honeycombed with secret spaces and dark recesses, and dense woods opening suddenly to magnificent vistas of marsh, sun, and sky.

So I begin on Alms House Road (a reminder of what constituted social safety nets in the days before Medicare and Social Security), an old dirt road leading to the southwest. The narrow lane is bordered by an impenetrable wall of viburnum, highbush blueberries, wild grape, honeysuckle (its fruit now turned red), poison ivy, and cascades of catbrier. Arching above the shrubbery and over the road are some relatively exotic trees: big-tooth cottonwood, buckeyes, and some of the largest black cherries on the Cape, 40 feet high or more. There are occasional clearings where beach plum mixes with the wild grapes and bayberry, creating a richly perfumed landscape.

In several places the trail skirts abandoned cranberry bogs, crossing their connections to the marsh on earthen dikes and wooden bridges. It is likely these bogs were "reclaimed" from portions of the salt marsh by the building of dikes — a fairly common practice on the Cape, especially in the heyday of cranberry growing. Now the dikes have been breached and a tidal flow has resumed into the old bogs, so that the salt marsh is reclaiming its former territory.

To the east of one of the bogs a series of old farmhouses sits picturesquely along a rise of land. East of another bog a connecting trail leads to the extensive "Ancient Cemetery" on Center Street. Here you can spend a couple of hours wandering through some of Yarmouth Port's oldest graves, which probably include many of the men, women, and children who made, tended, and picked these old bogs.

To the west of the bogs is a stretch of open pine woods. Much of the topography here has a "dug" or altered look. Off to the left is a long, low dirt wall, a sort of poor or lazy man's stone wall made of mounds of dirt with small stones imbedded in them like a plum pudding. There are several large, overgrown pits, no doubt the remains of "sand barrows" from which sand was dug and carted onto the bogs as a means of weed control.

Much of this area, then, shows signs of having been what landscape historians call a "working landscape," in which case, I suppose, it should now be referred to as a "retired landscape." But the ongoing biological processes so evidently and vigorously at work here reject any such anthropocentric terminology. In fact, "recovering landscape" might be a more accurate term, literally as well as figuratively, as forest succession once more takes hold and reclothes these human-made scars.

At one point there is a side path off to the right of the main trail leading to a shaded lookout at the marsh edge. A wide expanse of salt marsh spreads beyond the tree line and the shade, and you can see, from right to left, all the way from the tip of Dennis' Chapin Beach to the east, to the tern colony at Gray's Island in the center of the marsh, to the tip of Barnstable's seven-mile-long Sandy Neck, to the hills of the Barnstable mainland to the west, and finally to a glimpse of the spire of the Yarmouth Congregational Church.

It is a magnificent vista, all the more so for having come to it through heavily shaded and relatively enclosed walkways. The spirit soars to be suddenly given so much space and light and expanse. At this time of year the marsh is just beginning to hint at its late-summer/early-fall tawniness. A hundred years ago you would likely have seen out on the marsh a few staddles, or wooden platforms, on which salt hay harvested for cattle was stacked to dry, an ancient practice that persisted into the early part of the last century. Now there are still small flocks of terns hovering over the colony site, showing that these birds use it even this late in the season as a staging area before migration.

Far to the west the tip of Sandy Neck, Barnstable's seven-mile-long barrier beach, shows quite clear, with its topless lighthouse and the community of old summer cottages. There is a story of a nineteenth-century traveler from the mainland who set out on foot to walk the entire length of the Cape, took a wrong fork in Sandwich, and walked out to the end of Sandy Neck, thinking he had reached Provincetown. Today, I can believe it.

In the southwest corner of the property is an older forest with many sizable white pines, including one old monarch nearly two feet in girth, split into a multitrunked candelabrum. Then, just after coming up a short series of wooden steps, if you are watchful, you will find an unexpected botanical rarity: clusters of surviving sprouts of that vanished monarch of the Eastern hardwood forests, the American chestnut.

I have only infrequently found chestnut sprouts on the Cape, sometimes confusing them with chestnut oaks. But these sprouts have the elegant, long, dark green, hook-tipped leaves of the true chestnut. You probably know the story: how the American chestnut, a magnificent tree that grew up to eight feet in width, once constituted as much as one-third of the original Eastern forests. It was a valuable lumber tree, extremely durable, and the nuts were an important source of food, or mast, for wildlife, including the once-abundant/now-extinct passenger pigeon. The nuts were said to be sweeter than the imported Italian chestnuts we roast now, and chestnut gathering was a popular New England fall activity.

Chestnuts were virtually wiped out by the chestnut blight, a fungus that ecologists believe was brought over with imported Chinese chestnuts sometime before 1904. In fact, the present dominance of oak in our forests is due to the demise of the chestnut. The blight was the first of the numerous imported diseases and exotic invasive plants that have killed or displaced so many native species over the past century. Within a few decades the blight had killed virtually all of the chestnuts in the East, leaving the forest studded with giant dead hulks, whose rot-resistant trunks can still occasionally be found standing. There is at least one modest example of this among these sprouts here: an old dead trunk whose truncated form still stands nearly 30 feet high. But though the blight killed the trees, many of the roots remained alive, and for generations now they have been sending up fresh sprouts. Some of these even manage a few fruitings of the once-gathered nuts, but soon the blight hits and the sprouts once again die down to the roots. Still, though the role of the American chestnut has been largely consigned to environmental history books, here, and in numerous other spots, this mighty ecological drama continues: the persistence of life in the

DIRECTIONS

From Exit 8 on Route 6, take Union Street north to Route 6A in Yarmouth, turn left, and take your second right, Center Street. Approximately 1 mile on, turn left on Alms House Road. The parking area is immediately on your right. Other parking areas are at the end of Center Street at Gray's Beach and off Homers Dock Road. Maps of the Callery-Darling Conservation Area and other Yarmouth nature trails can be obtained from the Yarmouth Conservation Department at 597 Forest Road, South Yarmouth, MA 02664, or the Yarmouth Conservation Trust, P.O. Box 376, Yarmouth Port, MA 02675.

chestnut roots against the virulence of the blight still carried in its system.

One spring a few years ago, I spent some time walking through the hills of Tuscany through solid forests of European chestnuts, which carried more resistance to the blight and have largely recovered. The blossoms created a canopy of creamy clouds overhead, and the forest was full of the ruins of old stone huts where the nuts were once roasted and ground into flour. Never before had I been able to imagine what it must have been like to walk through the endless chestnut forests described by the old American naturalists. But that experience in Tuscany, coupled with the undefeated tenacity of these local sprouts, give me hope that someday, if not I, then my children or grandchildren, may once more go a-nutting for chestnuts in September.

A Refuge of Eccentricity.

WHEN HENRY DAVID THOREAU PASSED THROUGH Yarmouth Port by stagecoach in October 1849, he gave the village short shrift, taking only the following cheap shot: "We understood that a woman was the post-mistress, and they said that she made the best one on the road; but we suspected that the letters must be subjected to a very close scrutiny there."

Given Thoreau's eye for the eccentric, it is surprising that he was not more appreciative of Yarmouth Port, for more than most Cape communities, the village has always had a certain architectural and institutional quirkiness. Even today, such eccentric features as its dozens of old half-Capes along Main Street, the inimitable Jack's Outback (the hangout of the late Edward Gorey, who was himself no slouch in the quirkiness department), the idiosyncratic pleasures of Ben Muse's Parnassus Books, and the freshly oiled floors and old pharmaceutical furnishings of Hallett's Drug Store give Yarmouth Port an individuality of character that even those of us who don't live there can appreciate and derive satisfaction from.

One of the village's less visible local eccentricities lies directly behind the Yarmouth Port Post Office on Route 6A, and until recently it bore a somewhat misleading name. For years I passed by the sign that indicated the "Yarmouth Botanical Trails," thinking that it probably had nothing more to offer than a few acres on which the members of the local garden club displayed their horticultural talents. Perhaps I was not the only one who had this misapprehension, for a few years ago the name was changed to the "Historical Society of Old Yarmouth Nature Trails," which suggests, more accurately, an intriguing combination of cultural and natural attractions.

The property sits just outside the village center. In addition to some 50 acres of wooded uplands, wetlands, old pasture, and a small pond, it also includes the historic Bangs-Hallett House and the Kelley Chapel, an 1873 structure originally built in South Yarmouth and moved to its present site in 1960. Along its trails, at all seasons, one can hear traffic along Strawberry Lane to the east and Route 6A to the north, watch and listen to planes approaching the Hyannis airport overhead, and even hear the rumble of the occasional freight train along the rail lines that run along the southern edge of the property. Thus the woodlands form a kind of village refuge which few towns possess, a core of open space near the center of the community, a true and substantial "green heart," quietly beating against the encroaching world of mechanized transportation.

It was a beautiful day in early June that I first methodically investigated this property. Along Route 6A the clarinet-brush stalks of wild cherry blossoms and the pendant white spires of locust flowers were suddenly out everywhere. I parked behind the post office, picked up a trail guide, and deposited my 50-cent donation. The woods at first appeared to be an unremarkable mixture of pine and oak with a few hollies and white pines scattered throughout. The main trail gradually moves from the more cultivated plantings near the entrance — some English oaks, old apple trees, a Norway maple,

some grapevines, and one large flowering pear tree — to a more wild landscape. But even in the deeper woods the trails were lined with planted rhododendrons in full bloom. Most were deep fuschia in color, but occasionally a blossom of nearly albino white glowed softly among the dark foliage, and in one place I encountered a variety of rhododendron I had never seen before: a small bush with heavily veined small leaves and blossoms of mixed butterscotch and pinkish yellow.

There were numerous signs of an earlier, much more open landscape: patches of tall broom crowberry (or heather broom), some very tall bayberry bushes, a few open remnants of bearberry, some gray birch, and a large Norway spruce whose branches stretched nearly to the ground, suggesting that it originally grew in an open field. On the west portion of the trail is an open area perhaps 150 feet long and 40 feet wide, a transition patch containing much broom, bearberry, huckleberry, and blueberry, though it is gradually being invaded by oak saplings. I was delighted to read in the trail guide that this is "a remnant of a golf course fairway abandoned in the late 1920s." After all, if even golf courses may in time be swept back into nature's bosom, why not airports, malls, industrial parks, highways, suburban sprawl, Wal-Marts, and cell phone towers?

The most unusual and impressive natural feature on the property is actually not on the nature trails. Between the parking area and the Bangs-Hallett House stands an enormous European weeping beech, unquestionably the most impressive tree on Cape Cod, yet known to relatively few. In summer, from the outside, it appears like a towering cataract of green, resembling those mounds of kudzu that inundate entire trees in the South. During the cold months its dense, leafless canopy forms a stunning arterial kinetic sculpture against the winter sky. What a presence to have in one's backyard! What effects did it have on all those Bangs-Hallett children?

When you go inside it (and you do go *inside* it), it is like entering some colossal verdant circus tent. Like a circus, there seem to be more things going on at once than your eye can take in. Animal metaphors come tumbling down out of its soaring vegetable infrastructure of limbs, branches, and twigs: Its trunk is a gigantic elephant's foot that rises and metamorphoses into a fantastic green octopus overhead. The tree's soaring, spreading, plunging form creates a heady display of daredevil spiraling and lunging, death-defying leaps of limbs that scoop down to the ground and swoop back up again with a vertiginous giddiness. It has a mythic scope and vitality, like the Yggdrasil, or World-Tree of Norse mythology, which holds all of creation together.

Such are some of the general and specific features of the Historical Society of Old Yarmouth Nature Trails. Unusual and impressive as some of them are, however, they are largely ones that any visitor can experience on any given day. But what makes any of these local con-servation areas truly special are those unlooked-for, unanticipated intersections between the place and the visitor which cannot be found in trail guides, which are unscheduled and unschedulable. Such experiences are particular to the day, the hour, the moment. I was granted one such moment on my first visit there.

At the southern end of the property is the Pond Trail, which loops around Miller Pond and then rejoins the main trail. Miller Pond is a small, shallow, elliptical kettle pond about one-fifth mile long. On the east side of the pond is a small wooden bench overhung with a small red maple. The water level was low that spring. Highbush blueberries, pendant with epaulet-like clusters of white blossoms, lined an exposed muddy shore that sloped gradually some 20 feet or so from the edge. The mud was covered with fine, short, bright green grass. As I stood there, shielding my eyes from the westering sun, I noticed, about 50 yards to my right, a large brown form rooting about along the shoreline. At first the light made it look as if it had a flat tail, like a beaver; but it was, in fact, a muskrat. (The muskrat does have a flat tail, but it is vertically flattened like an eel's.)

The creature was snuffling and rooting about, waddling slowly and deliberately across the mud in a hedgehoggy sort of way. It seemed unaware of my presence as it gradually made its way toward me. I stood stock still beneath the little dangling pockets of rose-colored maple keys. Then I began to walk slowly toward the creature along the spongy upper shore. Still it showed no awareness of me. Its fur shone warm, brown, and rich in the late afternoon light as it wad-dled slowly, groundhog-like, deliberate and unafraid, like a skunk, nibbling the tender green shoots of grass, alone on the pond with me. It was so hedgehoggy, so Beatrix Potter-y, so English! And then, when I was only 20 feet or so from it, it took a large clump of grass in its mouth, turned, and, with no sign of alarm or even recognition, moved out into the pond, swimming off slowly, trailing its smooth V of water behind it, continuing its waddling motion even in the water. It followed the north shore of the pond for 30 yards or so, finally turning into the shore, heavily concealed by overhanging shrubbery, and disappeared into what I presumed was its den.

DIRECTIONS

From the Mid-Cape Highway, take Exit 7 and go north on Willow Street to the intersection with Route 6A. Turn right and go 0.6 mile. Look for the entrance sign on the right just before the Yarmouth Port Post Office. The nature trails are open year round. The Kelley Chapel may be rented for weddings and special events by calling 508-362-3021.

It was one of those chance meetings, when, for a brief space of time, you are ushered into the private life of another creature, one whose total unawareness of you creates a strange and sudden intimacy. Suddenly the place you are in becomes not just another "nature preserve," but a world unto itself; or rather, an integral part of the larger world. You are suddenly and deeply aware, beyond imposed precepts, that in some profound and fundamental way you share this place, this pond, and, by extension, this world, with other sentient beings. Such moments cannot be taught, or even consciously prepared for, for they work on the level of recognition and acknowledgment that is nonverbal and instinctive, like the spontaneous apprehension of beauty.

I left with a greater respect for the wildness and individuality of these "botanical trails." How lucky Yarmouth Port is to have preserved this piece of land in natural transition adjacent to its communal center. I thought again of how — like Jack's Outback, Hallett's Drug Store, or Parnassus Books — this nature preserve is one of the true eccentricities of Yarmouth Port. "Eccentric" is a word that is commonly used to denote odd or unconventional behavior, but it also has another and, in this case, more relevant meaning. In physics, an "eccentric" is any revolving figure, such as the wheel on a camshaft, which describes an elliptical or reciprocating orbit. Its axis of revolution is not at its geometrical center, but it nonetheless keeps the center true. This nature refuge is, like its geometric counterpart, a true ec-centric — a word that literally means "out of the center," yet which paradoxically helps the center to hold, a still, small refuge of dynamic constancy against the centrifugal whirlwinds of human and technological change.

Whose Historic Landscape?

WHEN I LIVED IN WEST BREWSTER, I OFTEN
visited Crowes Pasture in East Dennis. It was the closest large conservation area within walking distance, encompassing 129 acres of
upland and salt marsh habitats bordering Cape Cod Bay and Quivett
Creek. Over the years I must have walked there more than a hundred
times, at all seasons of the year, and I was never bothered by the
apparent contradiction between its name and the terrain I actually
encountered.

From the parking area at the East Dennis Cemetery, a narrow, undulating dirt road threads its way out nearly a mile to the beach. For most of its length the road is bordered by a tall, thick, impenetrable wall of shrubs and low trees, including honeysuckle, highbush blueberry, catbrier, viburnum, chokecherry, bayberry, Virginia creeper, and oak. One feels enclosed by a tunnel of soft and varied foliage. It is, at any rate, hardly a "pasture."

It had, of course, been a pasture at some time in the past, as had so much of the Cape's landscape during the nineteenth and early twentieth centuries. This one had just kept its name. There are even a few tall red cedars that stand above the bordering shrubs, testifying to its previous state (cedars being one of the tree species that commonly succeed abandoned pastureland).

But it was its rich present rather than its unknown, grown-over past that had always attracted me: the shimmer of new cottonwood leaves in the spring breeze; the abundance and variety of birdsong issuing in stereo from the wild hedges on both sides of me; the little paths leading down to the salt marsh along Quivett Creek; the ripening blueberries and beach plums of late summer; the tapestry of close, vibrant, fall colors from the turning bushes; the ridiculously gaudy form of a state-stocked Asian cock pheasant, cackling loudly as it rose above the shrubs like a barnyard rooster; the tangled fretwork of bare twigs and branches in winter, revealing dozens of last summer's birds' nests, most of them abandoned, a few roofed over with grass and serving as winter condominiums for field mice.

About two thirds of the way out, the dirt road branches into several paths that lead toward the beach. One of the anomalies of Crowes Pasture is that the only mature forest on the property is a seaside grove of oak growing in a narrow band just behind the dunes. Perhaps those who pastured sheep and cattle here deliberately left these trees as a windbreak in the old days. Kept down by the salt-laden winds, these trees do not grow tall, but some are nearly two feet in girth and many of them have split trunks growing in vaselike shapes that are at once grotesque and graceful.

The beach itself presents one of Cape Cod Bay's grand vistas. Crowes Pasture includes over a half-mile of shorefront. To the east are the town-owned marshes of Quivett Creek, and beyond them, in Brewster, Wing Island and the Paine's Creek marshes. Taken together, they constitute over a mile-and-a-half of municipally owned shoreline.

Here begins the vast expanse of tidal flats that continue to widen as one goes east towards the "elbow-pit" of the Cape at Orleans. In places these flats stretch out over a mile at extreme low tides. A hundred years ago, they were covered with dozens of fish weirs, complex arrangements of nets strung on poles that were driven deep into the mud. At high water the currents carried schools of herring, mackerel, and other fish into these nets. At low water fishermen drove their horse-drawn wagons out to the nets on the flats and shoveled the catch into the beds.

The traps are gone now, though occasionally one will see a modern version of the fish wagon in the form of a beach buggy, foolishly (and illegally) driving out onto the glistening flats. More than one has been known not to make it back. For the rest of us, these tidal flats offer unsurpassed opportunities for exploring the rich, hidden littoral life of the bay. At low tide these vast wet plains are etched with a myriad of markings, both animal and human. Clam holes and periwinkle trails mix with our own footprints and the marks of clam rakes, tracing our own need for participation in a wider life. Tide pools have been carved into banks of peat along the shore, creating natural aquariums in which visitors can observe hermit crabs, slipper shells, mussels, moon snails, and other marine life. In summer, when the tide comes in, the nearshore waters are active with feeding terns, plummeting like tiny silver-gray daggers into the shallow waters after sand eels; in winter, rafts of brant, scoters, and eiders feed on the eelgrass and mussels.

Because of these extensive flats, the shoreline here is more sheltered from wave action than in other places. This has allowed a nearly continuous fringe of salt marsh to develop, stretching out from the beach as far as a hundred feet or more. This fringe marsh also helps to protect the beach behind it. But the flats do not protect either marsh or beach from severe winter storms. Much of the peat shows signs of having been broken up, and active erosion shows in the low sand dunes fronting the beach. From the shore, especially during winter northeasters, one can see visible evidence of the shearing power of the salt air on shoreline vegetation. The shaved tops of a large stand of tough, gnarled oaks form a graceful curve that traces the path of the winter winds as they have passed over the tops of these trees for decades, shaping them and being shaped in turn.

Perhaps the most striking aspect of this beach, though, is the one that has given it its local name: Devil's Beach. The western part of the shoreline is littered with an unusual number of glacial erratics of unusual size. Mostly granite, these boulders range up to eight or ten feet in height and look like rough modern sculptures, something, perhaps, that Henry Moore might have created. I do not know exactly why these rocks inspired the name "Devil's Beach"; there doesn't seem to be anything particularly malevolent about them, though I suppose it might have been devilishly tricky to land a small boat along this shore. It has been common, however, not just on the Cape but in most parts of the Christian world, a tendency to give the possessive appellation "Devil's" to natural formations that are unusually rocky, barren, prominent, or grotesque in a given area.

As I said, it was always the present attractions, rather than its speculative history, that drew me back to Crowes Pasture again and again over the years I lived nearby. But one spring day in 2000, on my first walk out there in some time, the past rose up in a powerful and unexpected form. About three-quarters of the way out to the beach I came upon what looked like nothing so much as a blasted heath. With the exception of a few dozen spaced trees, some 15 acres had been stripped of all vegetation. Actually, "stripped" isn't the word; it looked like the trees and shrubs had been gnawed off, as if by some gigantic browsing animal — Babe the Blue Ox, perhaps. Roots and the scraped remains of small stumps lay in a raw tangle across the land. And there, suddenly, was a wide open vista down to the bay that had not existed for decades.

I found the explanation on a nearby sign: "With funding from the Natural Resources Conservation Service, this abandoned pasture was selectively cleared of vegetation by the Massachusetts Wildlife Biodiversity Initiative in cooperation with the Town of Dennis." This had been done, it said, because "The state is losing old-growth fields and grassland habitats to forest regrowth and development."

The initial clearing, I later found out, had been done the previous February, using a pair of large cranelike machines known as "the Brontosaurus." The name is doubly appropriate: the machines literally chew up trees from the top down, not unlike the behemoth vegetarians after which they are named; moreover, a machine named after a prehistoric animal had been used to recreate a landscape from the past.

I talked with Brian Malone, natural resources officer for the town of Dennis, who told me that the state will follow up the initial

DIRECTIONS

Take Exit 9 off
Route 6 and drive
north on Route 134
to Route 6A in East
Dennis. Turn right
and go east 0.7 mile
to School Street. Turn
left, then take the
first right onto South
Street. One-half mile
ahead, just beyond
the East Dennis
Cemetery, is a small
parking area at the
entrance to Crowes
Pasture. Vehicles are
permitted to drive out
to the newly cleared
areas, but the road is
not shock-absorber-
friendly and is fre-
quently filled with
deep pools of water.
Visitors should be
cautioned that upland
hunting is allowed in
season; check with
the Dennis Natural
Resources
Department (508-
385-8300) and wear
bright clothing.

clearing with selective herbicide treatment and maintenance mowing. In 2003 the town will take over management with semiannual mowing. The aim, he said, is to create and maintain not a "pasture" but a coastal grassland with native grasses and wildflowers, now one of the rarest habitats on Cape Cod. One of the main objectives of the project is to try to reverse the dramatic decline of species that need this habitat, such as bobwhite quail, meadowlarks, bushy rockrose, sandplain gerardia, and various butterflies.

It seems a worthy experiment, an attempt to restore what Brian calls "disappearing pieces of the puzzle" of the Cape's complex ecosystem. After all, "letting nature take its course" is no longer a sufficient strategy (if it ever was) for maintaining the Cape's biodiversity, for we are involved in nature everywhere. Reforestation, for instance, is a natural process, but there are places where we don't want it to proceed unchecked. The original coastal grasslands, moreover, existed in part because of the occurrence of periodic wildfires. But we have adopted fire suppression as public policy, thus generating the need to artificially re-create "natural" habitats such as the "new" Crowes Pasture.

We have decided that we want to "turn back the clock" to restore some of these vanishing landscapes for a complex of historic, aesthetic and ecological reasons. There is nothing wrong with this, as long as we recognize that it is arbitrary and reflects current human preferences rather than absolute environmental criteria. Why, for instance, this historic landscape? Why not one that existed 200, 400, 10,000 years ago? And why try to preserve these particular endangered species, rather than others that might thrive in a different altered environment?

Moreover, broad management goals — such as restoring or reintroducing endangered native species — could have unforeseen complications if taken to certain logical conclusions. Take coyotes, for instance. (Please take them, some of my neighbors would say.) One recent theory based on DNA analysis of coyote road kills suggests that these recent and controversial arrivals to the Cape may, in fact, not be "coyotes" at all, but Eastern Canadian wolves, the same animals that the first European settlers on the Cape encountered and rapidly extirpated. If so, then our coyotes could be regarded as having originally been "native species." Would that give them as legitimate a claim as piping plovers and wild turkeys to re-establish themselves on Cape Cod?

As I say, such proposed habitat management projects are worthy, and to some degree necessary, experiments. But it behooves us to recognize that our current priorities for managing open spaces like Crowes Pasture are as rooted in human desires as was the land clearing that originally created it.

We might also do well to recognize that nature does not so easily cede land that she has reclaimed as the sound and fury and the immediate victories of our machines might lead us to believe. The following November I returned to the cleared acreage and found, in the place of the blasted heath, not a renewed grassland, but an overgrown expanse of oak and cherry sprouts several feet high. Their red, gold, russet, and scarlet hues burned across my eyes like a prairie on fire.

The Two Worlds of Bell's Neck.

THE FIRST THING THAT IS LIKELY TO STRIKE A
visitor to the Harwich Conservation Lands is that most of it is not
"land" at all, but open water, swamp, tidal creeks, and salt marsh. This
area, in fact, is part of Harwich's Herring River system that, with its
tributaries, comprise one of the largest and longest freshwater systems
on the Cape. Fed by at least eleven ponds, it drains not only most of
Harwich's landmass but substantial parts of Brewster to the north.

At the head of the tidal reach of the Herring River, about a mile north of Route 28 in West Harwich, are two bodies of water that lie side by side, like twin ovaries, one salt, the other fresh, known as the East and West Reservoirs. Separated by Bell's Neck Road, their waters drain into twisting tidal creeks, joining together at last into the main stream for its final run into Nantucket Sound.

These two shallow ponds form the core of the Harwich Conservation Lands, a refuge encompassing several hundred acres, with many ties to the two worlds of freshwater and saltwater environments. As their names suggest, neither of these water bodies is natural. During the early part of the last century, the East Reservoir, the smaller of the two, was a working cranberry bog, created by diking off a portion of the salt marsh. Now its dikes have been breached and it has become a shallow salt pond, once more flushed by the tides and lined with phragmites, or common reed, and Spartina salt hay.

The West Reservoir was created in 1929 when a dam and flume were built on its southwest corner to keep saltwater out of several nearby bogs. They also provided a freshwater reservoir for the town, a fish ladder for the river's considerable population of migratory alewives, and a water supply for flooding nearby cranberry bogs. In 1964 the town voted to acquire several hundred acres of bordering wooded upland and several of the cranberry bogs to the west, which it now leases out to private cranberry growers, stipulating that no harmful pesticides or herbicides be used in their maintenance.

The reservoir areas and surrounding salt marshes have become a Mecca for local fishermen and birders. Almost any morning one can find small groups of binoculared birdwatchers walking along the shores of the reservoirs on Bell's Neck Road and a few fishermen casting from the dam or from the banks of the Herring River for perch, sunfish, and big-mouth bass.

For wildlife enthusiasts the Conservation Lands have something to offer at all times of the year, but there is no richer time than spring. Though much can be seen from the many dirt roads and informal paths that border the area, the life of these shallow reservoirs and creek-threaded salt marshes are best appreciated from the water.

One morning in early May, I drove down Bell's Neck Road beneath a canopy of white shadbush blossoms and launched my small kayak from the east shore of the West Reservoir. As I threaded my way through numerous stumps and stubs of a former forest that was drowned decades ago, I saw that they served as little arks for tiny green plants that were sprouting from their rotting tops, the product of seeds deposited by the wind or perching birds.

I paddled into a shallow area of emerging shrubs just to the north, where a mute swan was sitting on a large nest of twigs and grass. It seemed appropriate that an introduced European bird should be brooding on an artificial pond, but I respected its aggressive nature, strong beak, and the formidable strength in those folded wings and kept a respectful distance.

I entered an area of open shallow water, where all at once the water began to erupt around me, little explosions everywhere among the aquatic shrubs. The herring were spawning. Sometimes a wet, scaly, iridescent back would emerge for a fraction of a second, but most of their piscine passion took place discreetly, below the surface. As I paddled through this area, my kayak would sometimes roll over some submerged log or stump and I would feel as if the lake itself were muscling me underneath the kayak, reminding me whose place this was, that I shouldn't get too presumptuous about it.

This is the time of year when there appears to be a painted turtle on every other stump, many of them posed motionless with a leg extended, like little black traffic cops directing bird commuters out over the pond. The surface of the water was covered with tree swallows that flung themselves, as if shot from slings, across the water in rapid arcs, chasing insects and encountering one another in sudden meetings and flutterings, little fights, little aerial arguments. Nesting boxes have been placed on some of the taller stumps, and there the birds would congregate in tight groups of six or eight, perched on thin horizontal branches like musical notes on wooden staffs.

On the northeast shore of the reservoir a dozen or so black-crowned night herons (or "quawks," as they are known locally from the sound of their calls) took off from a grove of pitch pines. As they launched themselves they voided trails of chalky excrement, a habit that in the South has given them their plain-spoken local name of "shite-poke" — "poke" being a Southern term for "bag."

As their more respectable name implies, these herons are night feeders and day resters. But I had disturbed their diurnal sleep, and I experienced a twinge of that old childhood guilt I used to feel when my father was working the "midnight shift" from 12 to 8 A.M., and my mother would reprimand my brother and me to "be quiet because your father is trying to get some sleep."

I began to feel as if I were in some "bird demonstration area," where everything would eventually show itself. A large osprey, recently returned from its Central American wintering grounds, came around a corner with a large white perch in its talons. A female wood duck, with her bright white cheek crescent, shyly appeared among some reeds. (The heavily forested shores of the reservoir provide excellent habitat for this rare Cape nesting duck.) A kingfisher, with its loud machine gun rattle, burst out of a bordering tupelo grove. Mallards with glistening neck feathers emerged out of the vegetative patches. Grackles, also in their iridescent plumage, went hopping and skipping from shrub to shrub. There were dozens of gulls, and several cormorants taking off from the water, their dark serpentine bodies elongating, the loud *flap-flap-flap-flap* of their wings hitting the water, and their webbed feet, as they jerked them back and forth on takeoff, making lines of patters on the surface like machine gun fire hitting the water. And, of course, perched everywhere on the bright green curved branches of Andromeda bushes were male redwings, huffing and puffing like little bellows to better display their brilliant scarlet shoulder patches.

As I paddled along the western shore toward the dam I passed a grove of beeches bordering the pond. Loveliest of spring leaves, their curled lime-green tongues whispered in the soft May breeze and revealed inviting beds of moss beneath the trees, where nothing else grows in their dense shade. The red maples, as if proclaiming their name, were in their red efflorescence and already forming clusters of small winged red seeds, while highbush blueberries provided a white fog of blossom along the shore.

I pulled out at the herring run (known as the Johnson Flume) and saw the alewives erupting again, though in a more orderly fashion here, up through the concrete locks of the fish ladder. In good years, the Herring River run is one of the Cape's largest. The flow of fish was modest that morning, but several people lined the ladder with nets and buckets, taking their allotment for bait or smoked herring or garden fertilizer. Herring runs are one of the oldest, if not the oldest, form of communal gathering places on Cape Cod, and though the materials have changed, the method of catching these fish has not altered significantly since the Archaic Indians took alewives in this river several thousands of springs ago.

I portaged around the dam and started down the Herring River into a new world, one dominated by the influence of the tide. The change from fresh to salt water is not as abrupt here as it is below other herring runs, however, as there is a considerable freshwater flow from the ponds above, especially this time of year.

In fact, right below the dam the water was still quite fresh to the taste and the shoreline vegetation not that different from that of the reservoir, with freshwater shrubs, reeds and sedges, broad-leaved cattails, and tupelos and red maples coming right down to the river's edge. Only several hundred feet down the river did a brackish taste begin to creep into the water and broad-leaved cat-tails start to give way to the more salt-tolerant narrow-leaved variety. Gradually the river widened and I floated on an outgoing tide bordered by grassy seas of pure salt marsh. Along the broad, stately, winding course of the river I came upon at least two more swan nests and a couple of Canada goose nests, several more kingfishers, two large great blue herons taking off the marsh, and a snowy egret in breeding plumage, standing like a statue of an avian bride among the emerging Spartina grasses.

Such abundant natural beauty can create the impression that an area such as this is more protected than it actually is, until an unexpected human intrusion disabuses us of the illusion. At one of the southern bends of the river, beyond the Bell's Neck bridge, a large new house on one of the marsh islands along North Road suddenly came into view. It was a vivid reminder that spectacular areas like Bell's Neck attract not only wildlife and wildlife observers but also expensive new development along its edges. I learned later that there are several large parcels of private undeveloped land on the periphery of the Bell's Neck area that the town of Harwich has ear-marked for possible acquisition, using funds from the new Land Bank legislation.

A more welcome manifestation of unexpected residents along this stretch came when I paddled under the new, pressure-treated wood bridge at Bell's Neck and was suddenly buzzed by dozens of barn swallows dipping in and out from beneath the bridge where they

DIRECTIONS

From Harwich center, travel west on Great Western Road for 2.0 miles, then south on Bell's Neck Road approximately 0.4 mile to the isthmus between the two reservoirs. Canoes and small boats can be launched from here. To get to the herring run, go another 0.5 mile west on Great Western, turn south on Depot Road, then go 0.6 mile south to an unmarked dirt road on the left just before mailbox #494. A sign for the Harwich Conservation Lands is a few hundred feet in, leading to the herring run. The Cape Cod Rail Trail bike path also runs along the northern border of the Conservation Lands.

had built a number of their mud nests. With their dark, rich blue backs, cinnamon-colored breasts and deeply forked tails, barn swallows are easily told from the more common tree swallows. With the disappearance of old barns and other outbuildings on the Cape, their numbers have been declining in recent decades, and it was encouraging to discover their ability to colonize new structures such as this one, especially since the bridge designers, like the old barn builders, probably did not have these birds in mind.

When I got to the North Road bridge, I hauled out at the landing where two men were fishing for schoolies, or young striped bass, that come up the river this time of year — a catch and release sport. One of them told me there are also brown sea-run trout in this river, but they weren't going for them today. I left my kayak at the landing and walked back for the car. When I had set off two hours before, the East Reservoir had been a stretch of shining mud flats. Now the incoming tide had filled it up to the brim, and I was tempted to re-launch my canoe and explore it, too. But I had had more than enough for one outing, and so, like the fishermen, I decided to leave that one for another day.

Beach Plums, Beetlebungs, and Buried Wetlands.

FINDING AN UNCROWDED, FREE, PUBLIC SALTWATER beach in July and August is a common fantasy of summer visitors to the Cape, one that has become increasingly difficult, if not impossible, to fulfill. But at Brewster's Spruce Hill Conservation Area, an easy 10-minute walk will bring you to just such a place: a 600-foot town-owned sand beach on Cape Cod Bay.

Spruce Hill is one of the better-kept secrets of the Lower Cape, and the beach is only one, if perhaps the most obvious, of its many rewards. Purchased from the Castiglione family in 1985, the property is a long, narrow, rectangular parcel of land encompassing about 25 acres that stretches from Route 6A to Cape Cod Bay.

Its acquisition dovetailed nicely with the need of the Brewster Historical Society for a permanent home, and the nineteenth-century farmhouse at the front of the property now serves as the society's museum, which is open during the summer months.

Not large as conservation areas go, Spruce Hill nonetheless provides a textbook example of habitat changes from upland forest to open beach, a kind of cross-section of time and space in which bits of human history are interwoven with the warp of natural succession.

At the top of the drive off Route 6A, behind the museum, is a grove of tall, dark, planted spruces that has given the property its name and which serves as a parking area for visitors. The trail to the beach begins here and slopes gently and evenly down to the bay along an old dirt road. The first part of the trail runs through a fairly mature mixed oak and pitch pine forest, with an occasional beech tree here and there. These woods, if left undisturbed, may eventually become a "climax" forest where oak and beech will dominate. The soil is clayey and stony here; in fact, there are so many small stones in the road that you suspect them of having been placed there, which they may have been.

Just a few hundred feet down the trail a cyclone fence begins on the left, marking the boundary between Spruce Hill and the Cape Cod Sea Camps, one of the oldest continuously operating camps on Cape Cod, and one of a very few left of the many sailing camps that lined the Cape's summer shores only a few decades ago. Spruce Hill, in fact, was once sandwiched between two sailing camps, Wono and Monomoy. Camp Wono, the girls' camp, operated on the site of the present Cape Cod Sea Camps property to the west, and Camp Monomoy, the boys' camp, was situated on property to the east.

Apparently at some point the camps or the Castigliones constructed wire fences along both the east and west boundaries to prevent unauthorized visitations between campers at the two institutions. But adolescent urges are not so easily discouraged, and I remember, years ago, coming upon large holes that had been cut in both fences. In the late 1980s the Commonwealth purchased the Camp Monomoy property, which is now part of Nickerson State Park, and Wono and Monomoy merged, in this more liberal age, into what is now the coed Cape Cod Sea Camps.

As you continue down the trail toward the bay, you can take a side loop trail off the right that winds over to the eastern end of the property and then returns to the main trail. Gradually you will begin to notice that the pitch pines are becoming the dominant tree and the oaks have been relegated to the understory, indicating that this is a younger forest. Occasional scatterings of pine cones line the path, along with the stripped cores of the cones, like small reddish ice cream cones, showing where red squirrels have been busy.

Viburnum, elderberry, poison ivy and other shrubs now begin to appear, and small junipers (or red cedars as they are called here), an open field tree, still survive here and there, their lower branches sun-starved and de-needled. Junipers are often an indication of former pastures, since the seedlings will stand repeated grazing by cows, then sprout up once the land is abandoned. Very likely a few cattle once browsed here in sight of the sea.

Closer to the bay there begin to be breaks in the oak-pine canopy, and here some junipers still thrive. At one point the loop trail winds around a large healthy juniper, suggesting that the trail itself may be helping to keep the tree from being encroached upon by other trees. Reach out and pick a few of the bluish-gray juniper "berries" (actually a cone with fleshy scales) that grow on its dark green branches. Crush them between your fingers and smell. If you are not a teetotaler, you may recognize the familiar flavoring for gin.

Now, as the loop trail rejoins the main path and continues towards the beach, there are more signs of reverse succession. The tree canopy is increasingly open, and small chokecherries appear, sporting racemes of small black fruit, juicy and slightly bitter, which make one of the Cape's most delicious native jams. Here, too, the first bayberry bushes begin to mix in, as oak and pine gradually drop out, and the junipers, having access to full sun, become the dominant tree. It is not just more sunlight that accounts for this change in vegetation, though. Increased exposure to wind and salt from the bay also affects the plant community, favoring more salt-tolerant species. The soil, too, has changed, becoming more sandy and dry.

Finally the trail emerges into a true dune habitat, and here, in late August, you will find one of Spruce Hill's most sought-after seasonal prizes: an extensive and abundant stand of beach plums. At the end of summer the fruit of these shrubs hang like thick bunches of glass marbles, decked out in varying hues of pink, red, orange, and purple.

Just before the beach, at the east end of the property, is an intriguing example of literally buried history. Here the land slumps down into a small depression, surrounded by impenetrable vegetation, in which there is a small stand of tupelos, or black gum trees. Tupelos are small trees with dark, deeply fissured bark, crooked horizontal branches, and small oval leaves that turn brilliant scarlet in early fall. Tupelos prefer moist sites, and their presence here suggests that this hollow, now heavily overgrown, was once an open wetland. In fact, the 1943 topographical map of Brewster shows a small active cranberry bog on this spot, which drained into the bay. Further back in time it might very well have served as a water hole for cows that once grazed this reforested pasture. Over time the blowing sand has gradually filled in this bog so that today only the tupelos signify the presence of this nearly vanished wetland.

(If you'll indulge me a short etymological digression, there is a story about one of the tupelo's older, local names that has always endeared it to me. In this region, and especially on Martha's Vineyard, the tupelo is still commonly known as the "beetlebung." This somewhat comical name derives from its dense, twisted grain, which makes its wood virtually unsplittable. For this reason tupelos were favored by the early English settlers for the heads of wooden mallets, or "beetles." One of the common uses of such mallets was to pound stoppers, or "bungs," into the holes of whale oil barrels. Thus, by one of those curious but not uncommon linguistic inversions, the tree that provided stopper-mallets, or bung-beetles, for our Colonial predecessors in time came to be known as the beetlebung.)

During this short half-mile walk you have traversed backwards at least a hundred years of plant succession, a journey from the dark shade of the spruce grove to the light of the open beach. But there is one final revelation to experience, one that looks to the future. Walk down the short flight of wooden steps to the beach and look to the east. Beyond the town-owned property, and stretching all the way to Namskaket Creek at the Brewster-Orleans line, is a remarkably undisturbed expanse of dune, coastal bluff, salt marsh, and barrier beach, made up of local conservation areas, state park property, and town landings, all of which (with the exception of three or four modest private beach homes) is open to the public.

DIRECTIONS

Spruce Hill is located in East Brewster on the north side of Route 6A (look for the small wooden sign at the entrance) approximately 1.8 miles west of the Brewster–Orleans line, just east of the Cape Cod Sea Camps. The unpaved parking area at the top of the drive holds about a dozen cars. The conservation area is open year-round.

All in all there is almost a mile and a quarter of protected saltwater coastline here in one of the most intensely developed areas of Cape Cod — a precious preserve for this and future generations, of which Spruce Hill is an integral part.

A Palimpsest Landscape.

IT HAS BEEN A TRUISM OF LANDSCAPE HISTORIANS for some time that there is no square foot of Cape Cod earth that has not been altered, directly or indirectly, by human action. Before the European explorers appeared, local Wampanoags cleared large areas for agriculture and burned hilltop ridges to keep hunting areas open. Early settlers cut down most of the original woodlands for fuel and building material within decades of their arrival, and during the nineteenth century the Cape's ancient white cedar swamps were cut and converted into cranberry bogs.

In the last century, before the implementation of wetland regulations, hundreds of acres of salt marsh were dredged for harbors or filled for development. Even the enormous granite boulders deposited here by the last glacier were broken up for road beds.

All this human alteration was more apparent a century ago, when much of the landscape was still treeless and barren, the results of overcutting and overfarming Cape Cod's fragile forests and soil. Even today, however, when most of the Cape has been reforested, the types of trees and plants that give our protected areas a pleasing "wild" look bear witness to their altered past. A pine and oak monoculture, thriving on impoverished soil, has replaced the once-diverse hardwood forest. Abandoned cranberry bogs have been succeeded by maple, not cedar, swamps. At the edges of filled land, phragmites, or reed grass — an invasive species that thrives in disturbed habitat — has begun to make inroads on our remaining protected salt marshes.

Today, of course, the ongoing juggernaut of rapid development continues to transform much of the Cape's remaining open space into something that would be unrecognizable to previous generations of Cape Codders. Still, few places so dramatically reveal the alteration of natural forms by human action as does the Frost Fish Creek Conservation Area in North Chatham, owned and maintained by the Chatham Conservation Foundation. It is a palimpsest landscape, like the old parchments inscribed on many times by human hands, each previous layer incompletely erased and still showing through.

The acquisition of Frost Fish Creek began in 1967 (one of the first acquisitions made on Cape Cod by a local conservation group), with additional gifts and purchases made over the subsequent years. Today its 47 acres encompass a remarkable variety of wetland and upland habitats.

The property's northern entrance off Crowell Road does not at first glance look particularly inviting: a high, locked chain-link gate draped with bittersweet sports a "WARNING: DEER TICK HABITAT" sign. But there is a kind of cattle-chute pedestrian access around the gate, which then takes you across a sluiceway that drains an extensive wetland to the east. Sixty years ago this was a large working cranberry bog. A quarter-century ago, according to a 1974 topographical map, the area was a shallow pond. Today it is a wet meadow, full of cattails,

phragmites, wetland grasses, and large highbush blueberry bushes that burst into flaming fountains of color in the fall.

The history and present state of this abandoned cranberry bog is a significant example of a human-altered environment, but it is not the most dramatic one. After crossing the culvert, you can walk a half-mile or so on a trail that runs along the east side of Frost Fish Creek. The "creek" is now a shallow wetland that forms a long, narrow, brackish lake, with Chatham's striking double red-and-white checkered water towers looming above it on Great Hill. The best views of it are in early spring, as later on a thick border of catbrier, elderberry, inkberry, red maple, shadbush, ferns, and other moisture-loving plants screens much of the wetland. There are some unusually large pitch pines along the trail here (one nearly three feet in diameter) as well as some oaks growing on the hillside in grotesque twisted shapes.

Given its name, it is likely that Frost Fish Creek was once a saltwater tidal creek where "frost fish" — a local name for tomcod, a smaller relative of the codfish — once showed up in the fall, or frost season. In addition, a herring and an eel run were both said to have existed here at one time. At some point, however, a dike and tidegate were built at the lower end where the creek empties under Route 28 into Pleasant Bay. The creek became a freshwater habitat, and ice was apparently cut here in the early part of the last century. Later, the tide gate ceased to function and the present brackish wetland developed. The creek now hosts resident mute swans, as well as flocks of black ducks, several cormorants, the occasional green and blue heron, and various migratory shorebirds and waterfowl in spring and fall.

Between the end of the creekside trail and Route 28 is a rather barren piece of scraped-over land that is not part of the conservation area but possesses an interesting environmental history. The scene here is strikingly alien and emphatically unnatural. A series of strange, small wooden sheds dot the area, and on a rise of ground on the far end looms a modern, industrial, metal-sheathed, windowless, unmarked building that is imposing and slightly menacing in its insistent anonymity.

Four decades ago, when I first came to the Cape, this was the site of the Acme Laundry Company, a large complex that handled the cleaning needs of many of the region's hotels, restaurants, and

DIRECTIONS

The easiest access to Frost Fish Creek is from Route 28, about 0.4 mile south of the intersection of Crowell Road and Route 28. Parking is along the side of the highway, and pedestrian access is allowed along the dirt cartway between the creek and the oil recovery facility. Access from Crowell Road is more difficult to find. Park in the parking lot of the Chatham Middle School. Walk across Crowell Road and down Meadow Brook Road for about 100 yards. As Meadow Brook Road swings sharply left, continue straight ahead down what appears to be a paved driveway but turns into a dirt track.

other businesses. In those environmentally innocent days, we took for granted the frequent sight of suds flowing out of the culvert from Frost Fish Creek into the lower end of Ryder Cove. The laundry's boilers were powered by #6 bunker fuel oil, and during the 1980s it was discovered that oil had been leaking into the soil on the property for a number of years. The state's then-named Department of Environmental Quality Engineering stepped in and ordered the laundry closed. The buildings were destroyed by fire in 1991, and the state required the owners to build the oil recovery clean-up facility that now stands in its place.

Environmentally, this is probably the most significant change that has taken place in this area over the past several decades, but it is still not the most dramatic or fascinating one.

As you head back north along the creekside trail, take the first path that leads up onto the wooded ridge that forms the spine of the narrow, half-mile-long peninsula that runs between Frost Fish Creek and the former cranberry bog. The trees here are almost all pitch pine, with some young oak saplings in the understory, suggesting that the activity on this peninsula was abandoned fairly recently. On the steeper parts of the trail, where erosion and rain has washed out some of the soil, the pine roots provide unplanned "steps" for the walker.

Finding areas like this, reclothed in native trees and foliage, is always a reminder of nature's enormous capacity to heal itself. On the other hand, as Wendell Berry observed, such layered, palimpsestic, human-altered landscapes also carry a certain sadness with them, a sense of deep scars.

From the ridge it is easy to see that the entire topography of this peninsula has been spectacularly altered, twisted, and gouged into something very different from the gentle contours of its original glacier-shaped form. At one point the trail winds up and around a large semicircular bowl that has a small grove of tupelos, or black gum trees, growing inside it. Further along, the ridge itself contracts to a narrow passage only ten feet wide, dropping off precipitously on both sides into a pair of large bowls that almost, but not quite, cut through the entire ridge. The effect is that of a miniature version of the famous Knife Edge Trail on Mount Katahdin, where massive glacial cirques cut into the flanks of Maine's tallest peak. In another place the trail suddenly dips into a short "saddle" between

After another 100 yards, look for an unmarked path on the right that goes through thick shrubbery. On this path, look for a wooden "CCF" sign tacked to a tree — the only indication that you are now on the Frost Fish Creek Conservation area.

Trail guides to this and other properties are available from the Chatham Conservation Foundation, 104 Crowell Road, Chatham, MA 02633, or call 508-945-4084.

two more bowls. The scale of all these mountain-mimicking features, of course, is only about one-hundredth that of real mountains. The "summit" of this ridge barely exceeds 40 feet, but the precipitous and extreme variations nonetheless give one a sense of alpine giddiness, though on much safer and less strenuous dimensions.

These unusual formations are the result of numerous massive sand-barrows, or borrow-pits, that were dug into both sides of the ridge during the last century to obtain sand to spread over the once-active cranberry bogs — a common and ongoing practice used to control weed growth in commercial bogs. Such sand-barrows are common in most Cape Cod towns, but nowhere have they more strikingly altered local topography than along this narrow ridge. Traversing these mock cirques, knife edges, and saddles, one could almost believe that these features were not the unintended consequences of an activity associated with a local agricultural industry, but rather were deliberately created by men (perhaps Scottish immigrants from Cape Breton) who longed for mountains and, not finding any here, decided to sculpt the malleable Cape Cod landscape into diminutive reminders of their rugged, highland homes.

Courtin' Talk and Global Beauties.

ON THIS BRIGHT, MIDSUMMER'S MORNING, THE shoreline of Baker's Pond resembles an installation by Christo, the artist who has made a career of wrapping buildings, bridges, islands, and other human and natural landscapes in a variety of fabrics. From a distance it looks as if a wide pink and magenta ribbon made of sheer silk has been carefully placed along the eastern rim of the pond, rippling delicately in the morning breeze.

But this is nature's artistry, not man's. On closer inspection, this shimmering ribbon is composed of thousands upon thousands of Plymouth gentians: large, lovely pink flowers with red-rimmed golden eyes that rise on impossibly thin stems two to three feet high. A light, but pervasive fragrance, lilylike, perfumes the air around them.

Confronting such shimmering abundance, it is difficult to acknowledge that the Plymouth gentian's existence is threatened, not only in Massachusetts, where it is a state-listed species of special concern, but globally as well. This species grows only along the peaty margins of coastal kettle ponds. Moreover, the plants depend on a periodic fluctuation in the water levels of these ponds. In summers with low water levels, such as we have had for the past several years, these perennial gentians bloom profusely along the exposed shoreline. During years of high water, the plants do not emerge and this period of dormancy allows the rhizomes of the submerged plants to reinvigorate themselves.

In his book *A Vanishing Heritage,* Cape ecologist Mario DiGregorio notes that of 61 known sites for the Plymouth gentian remaining worldwide, 45 are found in Massachusetts, and most of these are in Plymouth and Barnstable Counties. Protection of the shorelines where they grow is vital to their preservation. Their very beauty, however, is a danger to their existence, for who, seeing such a glorious display, does not want to gather a handful? But, as DiGregorio advises, "admire its beauty and fragrance, then go pick some daisies for the vase at home."

The presence of the Plymouth gentians was probably the most compelling ecological reason for the acquisition of nearly half of the shoreline of Baker's Pond in 1988 by the towns of Brewster and Orleans. When I first came to the Cape in the early 1960s, this pond was something of a local secret, a remote swimming spot, one of several still available then. It was remote even though it practically abuts Route 6. There were only a couple of older cottages on the shore, and access to the state fisherman's landing was a mile-long, bumpy dirt road that claimed many a muffler. But at the end of a summer's day, it was a place you could go and skinny-dip undisturbed, and in the evening hang out with friends around a campfire with only the stars for neighbors.

There also used to be a rest area off Route 6, right at the landing. Gradually, motorists who were hot and dusty and just wanted to jump in and cool off began to discover the pond and make their way to it. Signs didn't work, and eventually the state put up a fence, but that didn't deter people either, and so several years ago they eliminated the rest area altogether.

By the 1980s this once remote kettle pond was in danger of becoming yet another overdeveloped pond, its shores completely ringed with houses, its water gradually and insidiously growing more cloudy and polluted with septic effluent and run-off from lawns and paved roads. Already the road into the state fisherman's landing had been paved and lined with new houses, and a new subdivision sprawled around the pond's southern shore.

But in 1988 something unusual happened — unusual because Cape Cod towns have always had a tradition of stubborn Yankee independence and uncooperativeness, if not outright distrust and enmity, towards their municipal neighbors. Latter-day joint ventures between towns, such as regional schools and water systems, seem to stem from resource scarcity and budget concerns rather than from a true spirit of shared community enterprise. So it was something of a refreshing surprise when the towns of Orleans and Brewster got together to purchase nearly 44 acres, including virtually all of the remaining undeveloped shoreline of Baker's Pond, which straddles the boundary between them. In doing so, these towns helped to preserve not only a globally significant plant species, but one of the aquatic jewels of Cape Cod.

Baker's Pond is clear and deep, with sandy shores all the way around and water that stays warm enough to swim in late into September. One of the attractive things about it is that it has a very irregularly shaped shoreline. In this respect it reminds me of Walden Pond, for like that larger and much more famous pond, its numerous small alcoves and bays hold the promise of mystery and discovery that exceeds its actual size. Baker's has long been a popular fishing pond as well, for the Commonwealth stocks its waters with rainbow trout, and on a warm day in April and May there may be up to a dozen pickups jammed into the fisherman's landing parking area and dozens of hopeful anglers in waders standing out in the water.

Despite its nearness to the Mid-Cape Highway and the omnipresent roar of traffic, Baker's Pond strikes one as a quiet and serene pond. This is another similarity with Walden, for even when Thoreau lived there, a portion of Walden's shoreline was cut by the railroad track that had recently been extended out from Boston. Far from ranting about it, Thoreau wrote with interest, and even with some affection, for the railroad in Walden. I'm not sure it's possible to have an affection for Route 6 and its traffic, but it doesn't destroy the ambience of the pond — perhaps simply because, like the rail-road, it's been here for so long, too.

Although the two towns' properties are contiguous, there is currently no vehicle access into the Brewster portion and no trail map available for the visitor. The pond can be observed easily from a number of overlooks only a few steps from the Orleans Conservation Area parking lot, with several benches provided that invite quiet contemplation. The woods here appear to be a typical oak-pine forest, but look closely and you will notice something unusual: a stretch of fairly mature oak, and beneath them a scattering of very small pitch pine saplings, about four feet high. By standard ecological reckoning these pines shouldn't be here; they should have been shaded out by the oaks. It's as if they haven't read the textbooks on forest succession and don't know that they're not supposed to survive in such conditions. In winter one notices a lot of winterberry with its brilliant, red, mint-tasting berries and its low dark green foliage growing among the dead leaves. In spring one is likely to hear the long steady trill of the pine warbler. In June the fragrant pink flowers of the understory azaleas burst out before their leaves.

The property contains an extensive system of connected trails and dirt roads that encompasses nearly half of the pond's shoreline. Since there are at present no marked trails or guides, let me suggest one excursion. From the parking lot, you can follow a walking path that goes north through oak-pine woods as it skirts Baker's Pond Road. After several hundred feet you will come to an old dirt wood road; turn left and follow it west up and over a hill to the Brewster side of the pond. Such roads were called wood roads, not because they went through the woods (there weren't many trees a century ago) but because they led to family wood lots. Many local people owned these tracts of remaining woods, which were often far from their houses, which they managed and cut for firewood. A life-long native of Orleans, Rowena Myers, owned such a wood lot out here and once told me a story of the role that these lots played in local courting rituals. It seems there was a couple who got married in part because the wife was impressed by her husband's talk about all the wood lots he owned. Then they came on hard financial times, and the wife said, "Well, Charles, I think we're going to have to sell those wood lots of yours."

"Wood lots?" he replied. "Pshaw! That was just courtin' talk."

Eventually this wood road intersects another dirt road that comes in from the right. Bear left at this point. On the right the land slopes down into an extensive, shallow kettle hole. This kettle hole holds, not a pond, but a rather impressive example of another rare Cape Cod habitat: a white cedar swamp. The Brewster conservation land skirts the edge of the cedar swamp, which in spring is usually wet and full of the sound of frog calls. Cedar swamps are mazes of tea-colored vernal pools, often interconnected, depending on the water level. The tall, pencil-straight trees rise 40 to 50 feet from mossy hummocks, gradually tapering from well over a foot in diameter at the base. They lose their lower needles as pitch pines do, and so present a dark, shadowy, columned hall of shaggy pillars beneath the feathery tops of the trees. (I should confess here that, for several decades now, almost every time I've mentioned a cedar swamp I've parroted the old natural history chestnut that these swamps are the preferred habitat for the parula warbler, a lovely little bird with a bluish back and a golden chest, which builds its nest from the old-man's-beard lichen that grows from the boughs of these trees. It may be so, but I have to admit that in all my years on the Cape, I've never found a parula warbler nest in a cedar swamp, and I've only heard the bird anywhere once or twice.)

After passing a few private pondfront homes on your left, look for a turn-off where you will see a brown-and-white sign identifying the Town of Brewster Conservation Area on Baker's Pond. Take the trail into the pond and you will see on your left a small shallow pond. It is hardly a pond, more a mud hole barely 100 feet long that was originally a part of Baker's Pond and has been cut off by a gradual buildup of a sandbar across the former connection. This is a process that Barbara Chamberlain describes in her book, *These Fragile Outposts,* as the "hen and chicks" formation, where a big pond with smaller coves will eventually develop these little cut-off ponds around its perimeter. Two other outstanding examples of this process can be found at Cliff Pond in nearby Nickerson State Park and at Wellfleet's Great Pond.

On a sunny day in spring you are likely to see a half dozen or more painted turtles sunning themselves on a mud bar in the center of this diminutive pond. These little shallow ponds are perfect turtle habitat. Although I'm not aware of a name for this one, there are several "Turtle Ponds" on Cape Cod, so-called because they attract turtles so well. The water table fluctuates, but except in extreme dry spells there's always some water here.

Eventually you will come to a rise facing east and overlooking the pond. In the evening gulls fly in from the Orleans dump and gather in a circle in the center, providing a white iris for the blue eye of the pond. Below, lying out from the shore, there are great pine trunks that have fallen down into the pond in times of high water. Supported on their own bare branches like skeletons, the silvered trunks with their twisting grain suggest humanoid forms.

Unless you happen to have an assessor's or a topographical map with you, you are not likely to realize that, standing on the bluff overlooking the pond, you have in fact crossed back into Orleans, which owns a little slice of the shoreline here. You will more easily recognize some obvious signs of former habitation, including a small grove of bamboo (not a typical native Cape Cod plant) and dozens of jonquils. There was in fact an old cottage here when Brewster acquired the property that had been owned by the same family for three generations. There was some talk about preserving the house and outbuildings and finding a way to use it that would have some value to the town. I liked the idea myself, for it seems to me that if a structure has been in a place long enough, and if it has been inhabited long enough and benignly enough, it has earned a certain right to remain.

But open space tends to be managed by local conservation commissions, which generally have little interest in maintaining structures. And so — like the superb old house on the Kent Point property in Orleans — all the structures here have been removed, and only planted shrubs and flowers remain to attest that several generations of a family loved this place well.

DIRECTIONS

Take Exit 12 from the Mid-Cape Highway at Orleans and head west on Route 6A towards Brewster. At the first set of lights, take a left onto Baker's Pond Road. Go approximately 0.7 mile and look for the Baker's Pond Conservation Area sign and parking lot on the right. Access to the pond itself is at the state fisherman's landing a few hundred feet further on.

A Summer Place for All Seasons.

WHEN I WAS YOUNG, AND THE CAPE SEEMED young, too, Orleans was the town I most wanted to live in. One of its enduring attractions is that Orleans is more intensely penetrated by salt water than almost any other community on Cape Cod. Numerous coves, harbors, bays, salt ponds, tidal rivers, and other arms of the sea deeply probe and thread its landscape, so that it seems more a loosely connected fleet of ships at sea than an anchored landform. Kent's Point, on Pleasant Bay in South Orleans, epitomizes this sea-invaded quality, and the fact that Orleans has preserved such places suggests it is still a town worth living in.

For its size, Kent's Point is arguably the most beautiful piece of conservation land on the most beautiful body of water on Cape Cod (and you can extend the hyperbole yourself from there). Acquired by the town in 1988, it consists of a long, wooded, steep-sided peninsula jutting some 1200 feet out into the waters of upper Pleasant Bay. It is surrounded by salt water on all four sides: Kescayogansett Pond on the west, Lonnie's River on the south ("river" being a local term applied to salt as well as fresh water-courses on the Cape), Frost Fish Cove on the north, and the upper bay's main navigational channel, known simply as The River, to the east.

Though it encompasses only 27.7 acres, Kent's Point seems much larger than that, in part because of its unsurpassed water views, but also because of its superb trail system, which includes benches, picnic sites, observation platforms, and a handicapped access ramp to the beach built by the local Boy Scout troop. Imaginatively designed and sensitively constructed, these additions maximize the property's aesthetic resources and at the same time respect its fragility. One can spend a casual hour walking its various paths without ever retracing one's steps, and come away with the feeling that one has experienced a place of much wider dimensions that the official survey might indicate.

Walking out the River Trail along the south shore, for example, one catches glimpses of Lonnie's River, glimpses that widen as one continues along the Beach Trail towards the Point and which culminate in spectacular and long-vistaed views of upper Pleasant Bay. Here are soft, rounded headlands, studded with pines and separated by winding watercourses. Along The River the serpentine shorelines are strung with one of the architectural glories of Pleasant Bay: its old boathouses, with weathered shingles and painted doors, some still with short sections of iron rails leading down to the water. Looking south past Sargent's Point to Hog and Sampson Islands and out to the low, thin bar of the Outer Beach itself, one discerns the tiny abstract cubes of beach cottages perched like mirages on the horizon.

Along the Cove Trail, on the north side of the property, salt marshes and freshwater seeps punctuate the shore, providing foraging areas for deer, raccoons, brant, scaup, mergansers, black ducks, and other waterfowl. The trail looks out across Frost Fish Cove (which gets its name from a local term for the tomcod, a smaller

relative of the cod, which shows up in coves like this about the time of the first frost) to another wooded finger of land known as Cummings Point, where, on a winter's morning, one can often view the impressive sight of several dozen great blue herons roosting in the tall pines.

The Pond Trail leads to Kescayogansett Pond, a salt pond that is the entrance to Orleans' largest herring run and in summer provides snug harbor to numerous small craft. Along these wooded trails, in spring, you may also come upon one of the property's botanical treasures, the uncommon little lady tresses orchid, with its lovely spiral of small white flowers.

Kent's Point is perhaps best seen, however, on a bright, breezy fall day, when Pleasant Bay recaptures some of the feel and look of a generation or two ago, when only a few sails yawed and tacked on its soft surface. Then the pungent smell of dried eelgrass rises from the rock-littered beach, and the clear blue waters, sharded with sunlight, hurt the eyes with their loveliness. On such quiet autumn days Kent's Point does not seem like an expensively protected remnant of a vanishing landscape so much as a particularly exquisite part of what once spread its loveliness freely everywhere.

There is a special appreciation that adheres to many locally owned open spaces on Cape Cod, one that comes not only from their ability to remind us of what once was, but also from the knowledge of what they might have been. In the case of Kent's Point, its fate might have been that of yet another exclusive waterfront subdivision had it not been for the vision and generosity of its long-time owner, the late Charlotte Kent, who sold it to the town in 1988 for much less than its appraised value because she wished to keep it "as open space for animals and flowers and other growing things. I think there is very little of that left in Orleans," she wrote, a fact all too evident in the proliferation of new houses that can be seen along much of the rest of the bay's shoreline.

Much of the charm of places like this consists in what they evoke as well as in what they show. Kent's Point gushes, not only with natural beauty, but also with a rich sense of the past, and therefore of human continuity. Two overgrown bogs bordering the property indicate this area was once part of the thriving nineteenth-century cranberry industry. The land itself was farmed as far back as the eighteenth century, and along the Pond Trail are signs of this agricultural past in the form of tall spirelike junipers glowing with turquoise berries. Junipers, or red cedars, as they are commonly called, are a "pioneer species" seeding into former pastureland. There are also a couple of large old oak "wolf trees" whose limbs, spreading wide into the surrounding younger trees, once likely provided shade for the family's cows or horses.

On a winter visit, near one of these large oaks, I came upon a stand of tall "mystery trees," with light gray reticulated bark. They bore characteristics of cherries, beech, and poplar, but seemed to fit none of these. What were they? I was content to leave them unidentified that day; every place should keep a mystery or two to draw us back.

Until a few years ago, the Kent family home stood at the easternmost end of the Point. Like so many old Cape houses, this one began its life elsewhere. Built in the early nineteenth century, it was known as the Solomon Hurd house and was originally located at the western end of the property. When the Kent family acquired the property nearly a century later, they moved the farmhouse out to the point. A large shaded verandah was added to the front, roses and lilacs grew up over and around the house, and a workshop, artist's studio, boathouse, and rustic gazebo were built on the grounds. Over the years the Kent house acquired that settled comfortableness of old summer houses, and Charlotte Kent spent most summers of her long life out on the Point from 1902 until she died in 1998, just shy of her 100th birthday.

Following her death, various plans were put forth for the continued use of the house — as a museum, artist's retreat, or housing for a caretaker. But the Conservation Commission concluded that the costs of restoration and maintenance were prohibitive, and the old house and its outbuildings were demolished in the summer of 1999. Only a cement square at the crest of the Point, overlooking The River, marks the site of the gazebo.

Perhaps this was fiscally necessary, but it is nonetheless regrettable, for these structures and their ghosts were redolent of another time, calling up a slower and more gentle summer community along its still waters. In their presence, imagination could easily conjure up parties of half a century ago, romances that blossomed here, courtships that were consummated in proposals, birthdays, and anniversaries of long ties celebrated. Such old habitations remind us that

DIRECTIONS

From Orleans center take Main Street east toward Nauset Beach approximately 0.8 mile. Turn right at the Civil War monument onto Monument Road and continue south 0.7 mile. Look for Frost Fish Lane and the "Kent's Point" sign on the left. Follow Frost Fish Lane 0.6 mile to the Kent's Point parking lot. A large map at the entrance to the property diagrams the trail system.

the Cape's landscape is, to use Henry James's word, peculiarly "sympathetic" to human occupation. They also remind us of a more patrician society — so easy to criticize now in our more socially democratic age — which was nonetheless responsible for keeping many of our special places intact and undeveloped until we, as communities, finally came to appreciate their value and began to take steps to preserve them. Recognizing this, we ought to value such places as Kent's Point not only for their present beauty and glimpses of Cape Cod's less crowded past, but also for their ability to provide inspiration and templates for crafting a more appropriate occupation of our landscape in the future.

The Right Place.

— *"It seems that whenever people are given a free choice, they move to open tree-studded land on prominences overlooking water."*

No, that's not a piece of promotional literature put out by the Cape Cod Chamber of Commerce, though they would undoubtedly cheer its sentiment. Rather, it is an observation by E. O. Wilson, the renowned Harvard sociobiologist, describing a phenomenon he calls "the right place." In an essay by that name, Wilson argues that there is a universal preference by human beings for such a landscape, a preference he suggests was shaped by our two-million-year evolutionary history on the savannas of the African plains.

It's just a theory, but I like it, in part because it helps to explain the near-universal appeal of a place like Cape Cod, so much of whose landscape approximates this evolutionary ideal of "the right place." Moreover, if Wilson is correct and we do have an ancient genetic predisposition toward the Cape, there is an intriguing irony in the notion that that attraction is much older than the Cape itself. In other words, our glacial landscape of ponds, plains, and ocean bluffs, only a few hundred centuries old, is itself considerably younger than our desire for it. One might almost say that we, as a species, imagined the Cape into existence.

Be that as it may, one thing I am sure of is that few places on this peninsula fit Wilson's description of "the right place" more strikingly than the Wiley Park–Eva Nickerson conservation areas in Eastham. It's unlikely that many townspeople of Eastham are aware of Wilson's theory, but they unquestionably recognized the special nature of this place early on. The 44-acre Wiley Park area, acquired in 1968, was one of the first conservation purchases made by a local community with grants from the state's Self-Help Program and Land and Water Conservation Fund. The abutting 25.3-acre Eva Nickerson property was acquired in 1981.

Together the two areas protect a substantial portion of the shorelines of Great and Widow Harding Ponds and virtually all of Bridge Pond. One of the glories of these ponds is dense stands of swamp white cedars that fringe much of their shorelines. Some of the stands are composed of thin, spindly, close-growing trees; but others, particularly along the south shores of Great and Bridge Ponds, are mature groves with well-spaced trees over a foot thick. Once a common source of valuable lumber, widely used for its rot-resistant qualities as foundation sills, fence posts, and shingles, most of the Cape's cedar swamps were converted to the more lucrative cranberry bogs in the last century. Along pond shorelines where they survived, many were cut down to provide water views for summer houses, so that uninterrupted borders of cedar such as one finds here are rare today.

Since Wiley Park abuts Great Pond, one of Eastham's busiest summer bathing spots, I tend to visit this area after Labor Day and before Memorial Day, when the human presence has receded and parking permits are not required. Especially on a clear fall or spring day, the correspondences with Wilson's "proto-evolutionary

landscape" are compelling, though one is more likely to meet dog walkers, bird watchers, or mushroom hunters than a hairy bipedal hominid ancestor. The terrain is mostly flat or gently rolling, and the woods of Wiley Park are almost pure "pine barrens": open glades of tall, thin pitch pines with little undergrowth, through which slanting sunlight slides in shafts of golden, mote-dusted light.

A remarkably large percentage of Eastham is still covered with these open pine barrens, particularly its western and northern sections. Far from being a "natural" landscape, these woods are a direct result of Eastham's agricultural history. Long after most Cape towns had abandoned farming, the well-drained sandy soil of the Eastham Plains supported a thriving truck garden industry. Well into this century Eastham was famous for its strawberries, aspara-gus, and turnips. Even today one occasionally comes upon "wild" asparagus still growing in abandoned fields, and Eastham turnips, sweet as Wellfleet oysters, are still sold at a few roadside stands and in local grocery stores.

Because much of Eastham remained in agriculture until recently, the process of forest succession got off to a later start here. Thus pitch pines and locusts, which are the common species that seed in to abandoned fields, are unusually numerous in Eastham. Despite their artificial origins, however, these woods have a primitive, unspoiled appeal. Many of the trees are dead or dying, victims of the pine-tip moth, the turpentine beetle, or perhaps just old age. (Henry Lind, Eastham's natural resources officer, tells me that one of the dead pines on the trail along the shore of Great Pond was struck and killed by lightning, which left a streak still visible down its trunk into the ground.) They lie prostrate on the soft needle-strewn ground, or else half-fallen, caught in the limbs of their liv-ing brethren, with sections of their black scaly bark sloughed off, revealing the white, polished, bonelike wood.

On the south side of Bridge Pond, the Nickerson property contains a greater variety of terrain and tree cover, suggesting a more varied history. The woods at the marked entrance are, like those in Wiley Park, primarily pitch pines, growing on gently undulating land marked with ridges, mounds, and the soft, paired troughs of old wagon ruts. Beneath them are scattered young white pines, likely seeded in from plantings.

Further east the land rises, becomes more uneven, and supports stands of dark, flame-shaped red cedars. This species usually marks the site of a former pasture rather than a plowed field. Young cedar seedlings, unlike pines and locusts, can survive repeated grazing by cattle and sheep. In fact, in the few open field habitats still maintained on the Outer Cape (the National Seashore's Fort Hill Area being the best-known example) one can find, among the mown grass, tiny prickly red cedar plants, no more than a few inches high, which may be decades old. These hardy survivors bide their time, and once these fields are abandoned, quickly rise up and colonize them. Further evidence of a previously open habitat can be seen in patches of bearberry and poverty grass that still survive in the developing woodland.

At one point on the trail is the wreck of a great pitch pine. Its base is a clump of a half-dozen or so trunks fused together into a mass almost four feet thick, above which large dead limbs reach like crooked arms up into the sky. Its base is slightly canted, as if something gigantic had tried to pluck it out of the ground, so that it looks more like a shipwreck than a tree.

No conservation area exists in a vacuum, but this one bears a more direct connection to a wider world than most. On Herring Brook Road, at the southern outlet of Bridge Pond, is the larger of Eastham's two herring or alewife runs. Neither of them is very large, but I have always felt a particular affection for the Eastham runs. Unlike the Cape's bigger runs, such as those in Brewster and Bourne, Eastham's were actually created by its residents well over a hundred years ago by hand-dug ditches connecting these ponds with the bay. Herring Brook is one of these ditches, running a third of a mile in a direct line from Bridge Pond to Cape Cod Bay at Cole Road Beach.

Unlike most of the Cape's natural runs, this one has little head, and water must be carefully rationed over the spring and summer months if it is to last. This means that the wooden gates must be slipped into the locks at the head of the fish ladder and raised again when sufficient water has built up to allow the fish passage — sometimes twice a day. During years of low pond levels, the young fry may be kept impounded all summer. However, if fall rains replenish the flow, visitors may see a massive outflow of young herring lasting well into November. More than most runs, then, this one depends upon the constant care and attention of human beings to survive, thus somehow linking us more intimately to the fate of its fish.

This run also has a modest literary history, for it is described in Henry Beston's *The Outermost House,* in a chapter entitled "An Inland Stroll in Spring." Watching a small school of herring in this run nearly 75 years ago, he reflected on "Nature's eagerness to sow life everywhere, to fill the planet with it, to crowd with it the earth, the air, and the seas. . . . What conscious resolution of men can equal their impersonal, their congregate will to yield self life to the will of life universal?"

I visited this run, its ponds, and the surrounding woods on a brilliant spring day in April. There were no alewives that day, neither at the pond end nor at the town landing; only a solitary gull stood at the mouth of the stream, looking out in silent anticipation.

I returned to its headwaters and walked along the northern shore of Bridge Pond, where two young boys sat on a large pine trunk that had fallen into the water, casting their fishing lines, talking of nothing — the hope of the world. I continued on toward the spot where Bridge Pond is connected to Great Pond by a short, shallow channel. The shadows of the dark green swamp cedars along the pond shores pooled in the stream and on the soft needled ground, while the reflected sunlight from the waters played in flickering, liquid bands on the underside of the dusky foliage and the soft brown striped bark. A spotted turtle sunned itself in reptilian immobility on a piece of half-submerged plywood; and the floor of the forest gave off a pungent fragrance of newly warmed pitch pine needles.

Suddenly I was aware that the woods were filled with dozens of high-peeping little birds, flitting through the branches like small gray-green leaves, moving with a definite though staggered and erratic motion, as though blown along by a common wind. They did not fly so much as leap through the trees, flitting from branch to branch and bush to bush, alighting for a fraction of a second and then taking off again. They seemed peculiarly unafraid of me, often landing only a few feet away, and appeared more like insects, grasshoppers leaping through a sunny summer's field, than birds.

They were golden-crowned kinglets, chipper little birds less than four inches long with a bright yellow cap and a distinct white eye-

DIRECTIONS

From Route 6 at Windmill Park in Eastham center, turn west at the traffic lights onto Samoset Road and go 1.3 miles to Herring Brook Road. Turn right and go 0.4 mile to the Herring Brook at Bridge Pond. There is informal parking at the trail entrances on the east side of Herring Brook Road. The entrance to Wiley Park is 0.4 mile further north. A parking permit for non-residents is required from late June to Labor Day.

stripe. Kinglets generally nest only in northern New England, and spring migrants like these are rare, at least in such numbers. As they hopped from branch to branch they kept up a constant high-pitched chatter that may have helped to keep the flock together as they threaded their way through the thick pines. It is nice to have a new bird descend on you in such profusion, like a benevolent plague.

When I came to the short ditch running between the two ponds, I knelt down and for several minutes watched for herring. I saw no fish, but the wind and the sun ran over the shallow water as it flowed gently and steadily across the clear, sandy bottom. At my back the tiny kinglets kept up their high, stringlike choiring. On the opposite bank a dry row of last year's grass rustled softly like a silk gown.

All things about me seemed to be in motion with a light but fertile buoyancy, layer upon layer, tremulous with approach. Tiny black minnows darted in the stream. A small swarm of nearly invisible flies danced over them, and on the surface of the water floated a few red bud scales, dropped by flowering bushes lining the banks.

For a moment I, too, came close to dropping into that slow stream and becoming part of its endless, patient cycle. It was just a moment, but a marvelously contrived one, full of peace and companionship, which can unexpectedly materialize in such places at any time of the year. I looked up to the sky and the sun with simple gratitude for the day, but they shone too bright and hard and distant. I looked down at the grass where I knelt again, and felt some deep and ancient response well up in me, like the flow of water out of these ponds. The grass whispered beneath me. It said, *Here — here.*

A Neighborhood Retreat.

THIS SMALL, UNHERALDED CONSERVATION AREA IS tucked away at the end of an obscure cul-de-sac about a half-mile off busy Route 6 in South Eastham. It took me nearly 30 minutes to find it the first time I went, even with detailed directions from Eastham's natural resource director, Henry Lind. As I finally wound my way down Peach Orchard Lane, a new subdivision street lined with contemporary Capes, I thought to myself, "This can't be leading to a conservation area."

But it did, and I liked it immediately. The South Eastham Conservation Area (a.k.a. the Lamont Smith Property) is a perfect example of "neighborhood green space." Town-owned and open to the general public, it is used predominantly by local residents. There is a strong case to be made for the creation of townwide systems of such neighborhood "pocket parks," and in recent years several Cape communities have been using Land Bank funds to purchase just such small but significant properties.

Sometimes these neighborhood open spaces protect rare habitats or important views; sometimes they have outstanding aesthetic value, or historic significance. But they don't need these special qualities to serve their main purpose, which is to provide green spaces within walking distance of each neighborhood: places where local residents can find some peace and quiet among natural surroundings, take walks with their pets, do some amateur birdwatching, botanizing, or entomology, or, in the case of kids, simply engage in that crucial, and increasingly rare activity: unsupervised and imaginative exploration of a wood, a swamp, an old field, or a marsh island that can result in a lifelong bonding with the natural environment.

Though only 26.8 acres in extent, the South Eastham Conservation Area property harbors a rich variety of habitats within its modest boundaries. It also contains some unusual tree species, some striking evidence of how rapidly nature can reclaim an area, and an intriguing example of how we often mistake aesthetically attractive artificial landscapes for "natural" ones.

The woods here look at first like the typical Cape mix of oak, with some larger, taller pitch pines that are the remnants of an earlier forest. But on closer inspection I discovered that there are no less than five species of conifers on the property. In addition to the pitch pines, there are some young, understory white pines (one of the few evergreens that can survive beneath the dense shade of oaks), a stand of older red pines along the western edge (these nonnative trees were planted extensively as reforestation projects during the 1930s), and some struggling red cedars along the southern border.

But in the center of this small forest is an unexpected grove of a dozen or more mature larch trees, 40 to 50 feet tall, with some over a foot in diameter. Larches, also known as tamaracks and hackmatacks, are trees of more northern climes and are not native

to the Cape, though one occasionally finds them planted in local yards as decorative trees. They are lovely trees, with mast-straight trunks and fine, short, lime green needles that give their foliage a light, airy feel. Along with southern bald cypresses, larches are the only North American conifers that shed their needles in the fall. In October they begin to take on a glowing golden color that contrasts strikingly with the deep green of the oaks and pitch pines.

Larches also had more practical uses in the past, which may have accounted for this grove's having been planted by some former owner. Their roots are rot-resistant and often bent at sharp right angles, which made them a valued source of "ship's knees," or instep braces, that were used in making the hulls of small wooden boats. In addition, the early New England naturalist John Josselyn ascribed healing powers to the sap of the larch, asserting that it "is singularly good to heal wounds, and to draw out the malice . . . of any Ach rubbing the place therewith."

In addition to the conifers and oaks, there are some rather grotesquely bent tupelos, or black gum trees, which ring the small wetlands and turn brilliant scarlet in the fall. Tupelos have a slightly spooky quality to them; as you walk through the woods, they seem to peek out from behind the larger trees, almost as if they're being inquisitive, and then dart back in as you pass.

Even ordinary trees show unusual abilities from time to time. In one place on the trail I came upon a young oak that had grown between two straight pitch pines. It appeared to have been maimed in some way when just a sapling. At a height of about two feet it bent sharply horizontal; half of the lower trunk had been cut or ripped away but was now barked over. As the tree grew horizontally between the two pines, it split into two; one trunk grew straight up beside one of the pitch pines, but the other one maintained a horizontal orientation for another 15 feet or more before resuming its vertical climb.

I'm always amazed at the adaptability of these trees, their almost serpentine quality. I stood there for several minutes trying to conjecture the possible history that this frozen drama of growth suggested. Imagine if we humans left visible trails of our past to which we remained physically attached, so that we literally could not "leave our old life behind" and start over. A tree can head out in new directions, but it can never abandon its roots. Perhaps this is why we are so taken with trees — they provide a contrast to our own lives, which seem to grow more mobile and unrooted.

In addition to its intriguing variety of trees, the property contains three small ponds, the largest of which is barely 200 feet across. The one in the north end of the property is accessed by a small wooden bridge that crosses a drainage ditch, which drains the pond into the nearby salt marsh. And herein lies a fascinating tale of past human alteration of this land. If you follow the trail west 100 feet or so from the pond, you come out, rather unexpectedly, on the Cape Cod Rail Trail, where there is an open expansive view of a large area of salt marsh bordering Cape Cod Bay. Originally, the small pond and the surrounding wetland were part of this larger salt marsh system.

During the late 1860s, however, the Old Colony Railroad was extended into Eastham, and a track bed was constructed through the salt marsh here. The bed cut off this portion of the marsh from the tides, eventually turning it into a fresh or brackish swamp and pond system, drained by the ditch. On high course tides the pond is still occasionally flooded, reminding us of its saltwater origins. Though adjacent to and easily accessible from the Rail Trail, there are no signs or any other indication of the conservation area's existence from the bike path. Thus, ironically, those who use the path are probably unaware of this area, although it was created, to a significant degree, by the very railroad bed on which they ride.

In the southern portion of the property is a section of woodland that is labeled as "Fields" on the hand-drawn trail map provided by the town. I asked Henry Lind about this, and he said, "Yes, hard to believe, but when we acquired the property it was wide-open fields there." Now, only a dozen years later, it takes some detective work to spot signs of former field habitat: some large "wolf" oaks, multi-trunked and begging to be climbed, that spread their wide crowns over what was once open pasture; some dying red cedars that sprouted after the field was abandoned and are now being shaded out by the younger oaks; a few surviving strawberry vines, and even some small patches of bearberry that once thrived on an open Eastham moor.

The second of the three small ponds, at the southern end of the trail, is completely hidden from view by a thick wall of impenetrable catbrier vines strung from pitch pines and other trees, reminding

DIRECTIONS

From the Orleans rotary, head north on Route 6 for 0.5 mile and take your first left onto South Eastham Road. Follow South Eastham Road 0.2 mile until it veers right. Continue straight ahead onto Arrowhead Drive and take your first left onto Peach Orchard Lane. A small parking lot is at the end of the road. A map of the South Eastham Conservation Area trail system may be obtained from the Eastham Natural Resources Department on Old Orchard Road. Call 508-240-5972.

one of the bramble walls that surrounded Sleeping Beauty's castle. The third, and largest, pond, however, straddles the eastern edge of the property and is quite accessible. There is a large, old spreading oak tree and several tupelos right on the bank that provide welcome shade in the summer, a canopy of shifting green through which patches of blue sky peek. Here, beneath the chiaroscuro of shifting sunlight and leaf patterns, one can sit and listen to the muffled roar of summer traffic as it chases itself around the Orleans rotary like Little Black Sambo's tigers.

There is a private home on the far side of this little pond, but this little neighborhood park provides waterfront property for every visitor. Here one may rest and contemplate the pond waters, the reflections, what moves over it and comes up to its surface from below, perhaps even see deer or raccoon come to its edge in the evening or at dawn — for there are tracks in the mud along the shore. I thought of old Josselyn's comment about larch sap and how places like this are also "singularly good to heal wounds, and to draw out the malice . . . of any Ach rubbing the place therewith."

A generation or two ago such small places and the opportunities they provided were commonplace on the Cape, part of the daily experience of those who lived or visited here. They were taken for granted, and thus left unprotected. Now that almost every acre on this peninsula has been developed, is slated for development, or has been protected (usually in the form of large areas at some distance from most of the local population), the value of these neighborhood green spaces is increasingly recognized. One could do worse than look to the South Eastham Conservation Area as a model.

Wild at Heart.

IN A SENSE, ONE HAS TO BE AT WIT'S END TO VISIT Wellfleet's Cannon Hill. That is, the wooden footbridge that crosses Duck Creek to this island park lies at the bottom of Whit's Lane, where it intersects with East Commercial Street.

Bad puns aside, Cannon Hill, or Hamblen's Island as it is also known, was sold to the town in 1931 by Annie Hopkins as a public park, and thus may lay claim to being the first piece of dedicated open space in the town of Wellfleet.

As open space goes, it is of fairly modest dimensions, encompassing only 3½ acres of upland and some 8½ acres of surrounding marsh and tidal flat. The hill itself, a mound of glacial sand some 40 feet high, is connected to the mainland by a narrow footbridge known as Uncle Tim's Bridge. Its slopes are covered with an open forest of young, second-growth pitch pines, with a few junipers, cottonwood, and oak sprouts thrown in for variety. The ground vegetation is a spare and fragile mix of bearberry and grasses, and its topography shows signs of overuse and abuse, with several raw gullies and eroded trails scarring its slopes.

Still, it is one of Wellfleet's most popular destinations, in part because it is a visible and attractive piece of green space adjacent to the center of town. Moreover, its modest elevation offers a commanding prospect of the town itself, a place from which to stand and gather it all in in one sweep of the eye. It also offers, to the mind's eye, a remarkable perspective on two and a half centuries of the town's seafaring history.

Standing at the top of Cannon Hill and looking south, one sees the old railroad causeway and the ruined trestle that cuts across the lower part of Duck Creek. During the early nineteenth century, Duck Creek was Wellfleet's main harbor, bristling with "a forest of wharves." Schooners were built at Roger's shipyard, packet ships brought passengers and mail from Boston, salt was evaporated from sea water in salt works, and wooden freighters brought lumber from Maine, unloading it where the Nickerson Lumber Company still operates today.

When the Old Colony Railroad reached Wellfleet about 1870, the causeway and low bridge cut off large boats from access to the upper part of the creek, and ship traffic moved out to the site of the present-day marina. Wellfleetians, however, adaptable as any Cape Codders, built oyster shacks out from the railroad causeway and continued to pursue the town's most famous shellfish crop. The shacks and the railroad are both gone today, but the abandoned oyster boats lay in the mud of the old harbor for decades, giving rise to the local saying that "Old oyster boats never die, they just lie around Wellfleet Harbor." A couple of the rotting hulls still remain, and in a fitting irony, these wrecks have themselves become substrates to which young oyster spat now attach themselves.

Back across the foot bridge, fronting the shoreline to the west, is Commercial Street. As its name suggests, Commercial Street was the town's center of commerce in the early 1800s. Many of the old houses and structures that still line the street housed blacksmith shops, a cooperage, chandleries, wheelwrights, sail lofts, dry goods businesses, and grocery stores. Uncle Tim's Bridge is itself named after Tim Daniels, who operated a general store in the house that is now to the left of the Cherrystone Gallery. The present bridge is actually the latest in a long series of spans that have linked Cannon Hill to the mainland since at least 1783. All of the original businesses and most of the old structures are now galleries, cafes, and craft shops, catering to a different, but no less profitable, clientele.

To the north, across the marsh, the town rises towards Main Street, which became Wellfleet's business center in the latter 1800s. From Cannon Hill the town appears as a foreshortened jumble of old houses climbing up from East Commercial to East Main Street. The compact, serried ranks of roofs and gables look like a New England version of some Italian hill town, culminating in the dark, peaked, gothic steeple of the Methodist Church and the graceful, blue-green, bell-shaped cupola of the Congregational Church. Visitors to town are frequently confused when the Congo Church's bells ring the hours and half-hours, for they do so in ship's time, the only public clock in the world that does so.

This historical overview, as it were, has become increasingly obscured in recent decades by the growth of trees on the island. Surrounded as it is by water and wetlands, Cannon Hill might be a good candidate for "controlled burn" management; that is, the burning or removal of the trees and shrubs that would return it to the treeless, heathlike state that appears in old photographs of the area. Such a landscape would not, of course, be a "natural" one (though neither is the present one) but it would restore the unobstructed view described above and would constitute an "historical landscape," of which there are fewer and fewer examples as the Cape continues to reforest itself.

On the other hand, Cannon Hill as it is contains more natural attractions than might at first be apparent. For one thing, Duck Creek itself, though constricted and diminished by the railroad causeway, is still tidal, giving it a daily diastolic rhythm. At high tide the creek fills up to the brim, submerging the marshes and —

especially at moon tides — even creeping up into the lumber yard and around the stacks of boards and studs, as if it would float them back out to sea.

At low tide the marshes and dark mud flats are exposed, attracting numerous birds. This is one of the best places I know to observe greater yellowlegs: large, long-legged, long-billed sandpipers that wade in the narrow creeks at low tide, feeding on minnows and crustaceans. Their characteristic loud, three-note, descending whistle — *wheet-wheet-wheet* — identifies them at once. They are usually surrounded by the ubiquitous and opportunistic herring gulls, which wait for them to take a fish and then try to harass them into dropping it.

The upper reaches of the creek are a favorite feeding spot for black ducks, mallards, and other "puddle ducks"; and a resident harrier, or marsh hawk, can frequently be seen patrolling the bordering marshes for rodents and other prey.

Because the banks of Duck Creek drop off steeply on most sides (one of the characteristics that made it a good harbor), the marsh is composed primarily of narrow bands of cordgrass, the tall, stiff reeds that line the tidal streams. But on the back, or north side of Cannon Hill, is a wide swath of *Spartina patens,* or salt hay, the fine, delicate grass of the upper marsh that collapses into graceful curved swaths, or "cowlicks," creating the appearance of a frozen green sea.

On the creek banks, among the cordgrass, and along the sandy mud flats at upper reaches of the marsh bordering the park, you will see at most times of the year hundreds of small holes with mounds of excavated mud and sand pellets beside them. If you are quick in your approach, you may observe the residents of these burrows, the fiddler crabs — small dark crustaceans only an inch or so in width — scurrying out of sight. If you remain quiet and still, the crabs will soon reemerge and you will be able to observe one of the most fascinating of Cape Cod's natural residents.

Fiddler crabs are said to be the most numerous of all crabs, inhabiting salt marshes and tidal flats to a density of 1,000,000 crabs per acre. They dig their burrows down into the peat of the marsh to a depth of a foot or two. Here they quickly retreat at any sign of movement, and during every high tide. Such timorousness is well warranted, as fiddler crabs are one of the major sources of food for both marine and terrestrial visitors to our marshes and estuaries, including gulls, ducks, herons, and shorebirds.

On some of the steeper creek banks, the peat ledges are honey-combed with the exposed burrows of these crabs. This extensive excavation seems to accelerate the erosion of the very peat in which the crabs make their homes, much like the homeowners who build houses on fragile dunes or ocean bluffs, undermining the vegetation that holds these landforms together.

The most distinctive feature of these small crabs, and the one that gives them their common name, is the hugely oversized claw (usually the right one) of the male fiddler. Much speculation has been made over the functions of this appendage, but it unquestionably plays an important role in the crabs' courtship behavior. During the summer you can observe a group of males industriously excavating their burrows or feeding on marsh detritus. Then some females will crawl by, and the entire male population will suddenly stop its work. Each male will begin waving its large claw in a "fiddling" motion in the direction of the females, hoping to lure one to his burrow for copulation.

These large claws also figure as weapons in the many fights the males engage in during breeding season. Such pugnaciousness in their character has given our two most common species of fiddler crabs their specific names: *Uca pugnax,* "the fighter," and *Uca pugilator,* "the boxer" — though these fights seem more exhibitionist bouts than real mixers.

Rachel Carson suggested that the males' claw-waving may serve as a means of communication as well as attraction. At times, two of the males will face off, a couple of inches apart, pumping their bodies up and down and waving their claws in unison. Perhaps this is some form of ritualistic challenge, or perhaps, if they fail to attract any females, they are simply saving face by staring down one another. In any case, so little is known about crustacean communication that such speculation cannot just be written off. Like birdsong, the functions of claw-waving appear to grow more complicated the closer we look at them and should include at least the possibility of pure enjoyment: "If you've got it, flaunt it!"

Sometimes the waters around Cannon Hill are host to much larger and more problematic natural visitors, though ones that are hardly strangers to the flats of Wellfleet. In February of 1998 three white-sided dolphins (part of a larger pod of 15 to 20 animals) swam up Duck Creek above Uncle Tim's Bridge, became confused in the narrow confines, and were in danger of becoming stranded on the outgoing tide. Two of the dolphins were successfully shepherded back out through the break in the railroad causeway, but a third animal became trapped in the marsh on the back side of Cannon Hill and had to be euthanized.

It was this event — the appearance of these oceanic marine mammals in the shadow of Cannon Hill — that made me realize that Duck Creek, however altered and diminished by human activity, remains a vital and unpredictable artery, bringing currents of wildness up into the very heart of the town. Several of the Cape's communities have such a wildness at their heart — the extensive tracts of the Beebe Woods in downtown Falmouth, the Mashpee River corridor in Mashpee center, the little-known Boland's Pond in the center of Orleans, the untamed ocean itself now knocking at the front door of downtown Chatham — though we are often unaware of its presence. A place like Wellfleet's Cannon Hill affords not only a perspective on the town's long human history, but a place from which to see how, despite our ongoing attempts to set ourselves apart from nature, the human and natural worlds constantly intersect.

DIRECTIONS

From Route 6, take the turnoff at the traffic lights onto Main Street, to Wellfleet center. After 0.2 mile, take the first left onto East Commercial Street. After 0.2 mile, on your left you will see a small parking area for Uncle Tim's Bridge.

A Weatherbeaten Face.

A LATE NOVEMBER AFTERNOON AT THE HIGH HEAD Conservation Area in North Truro. Below the rolling, open bluffs that rise like frozen, grey, ocean swells above Pilgrim Lake, a thin line of cars, some with their headlights already on, crawls along Route 6 toward Provincetown at the beginning of the last holiday weekend of the year. The flow of vehicles is a mere trickle compared to the vanished flood of summer traffic, but Provincetown needs every infusion of tourist money it can get to survive the winter and the Cape's long, wet, cold springs.

Some of the cars are leaving town as well, heading for a Thanksgiving with off-Cape families and friends. They thread their way between the dense line of bayfront cottages, restaurants, and motels on their right and the broad, shallow, wind-chopped waters of Pilgrim Lake to the left. As they begin to climb up from sea level to the modest heights of High Head, I doubt that many of these southbound travelers give a thought to the open expanse of moorland here, on the right, stretching between Route 6 and 6A. If anything, they probably assume, as I did for years, that it is part of the Cape Cod National Seashore. Few will notice the small blue sign beside the highway that says "CONSERVATION AREA — 1000 FEET AHEAD," and very few, if any, this time of year, will actually pull over at the rest area, get out, and discover the true identity of this small gem of local conservation.

The High Head Conservation Area encompasses some 50 acres of mostly open moorland and low pitch pine woodland that was purchased in two acquisitions by the town of Truro, the first in 1985 and the second in 1997. In addition, a 29-acre well site, belonging to the town of Provincetown, abuts the conservation area to the south, creating a protected triangle of nearly 80 acres of open space and critical habitat. This is one of the few areas outside of the National Seashore boundaries where the public can experience an open moorland landscape: broad stretches of bearberry, or hog cranberry, along with patches of poverty grass, broom crowberry, lowbush blueberry, bayberry, beach plum, and other plants typical of this open habitat.

Moorlands once composed much of the dominant vegetative cover on Cape Cod, particularly here on the Outer Cape, but over the past several decades fire suppression, natural succession, and reforestation efforts have rapidly replaced open moorland with pine and oak. In fact, open moor or heath has become such an uncommon landscape in recent years that efforts are now being made in places on Martha's Vineyard, Nantucket and the Cape's Audubon sanctuaries to artificially maintain or restore moorland through controlled burning, shrub removal, and other management techniques.

Even in the summer this is not what most people would call a lush landscape, though it has a rich, if subtle beauty at all times of the year. In early May the beach plums have their two weeks of white glory, and in June the low mounds of poverty grass (named because

it grows in poor soil where other plants cannot) light up with brilliant tiny yellow flowers. The stiff and fragile carpet of bearberry is ripped in places by sand blowouts, and in early summer the annual infestation of web worms tends to defoliate the beach plums — though this in turn makes High Head an excellent spot to catch a glimpse of the uncommon black-billed cuckoo, a major predator of these caterpillars instantly recognizable by its repeated hollow wooden call: *cu–cu–cu–cu.*

In September the patches of blueberry take on the color of glowing embers, but by late autumn even these modest hues have vanished, and the moor presents a sere and bleak prospect to the visitor. The bearberry has taken on its dark wine-colored winter tones; the poverty grass has become grey, ragged mops; the shrubs are leafless. The scene, in fact, evokes William Bradford's vivid description of this part of the Cape when the little band of Pilgrims first came ashore 379 Novembers ago:

And for the season it was winter, and they that know the winters of that country know them to be sharp and violent, and subject to cruel and fierce storms, dangerous to travel to known places, much more to search an unknown coast. Besides, what could they see but a hideous and desolate wilderness, full of wild beasts and wild men . . . for which way soever they turned their eyes (save upwards to the heavens) they could have little solace or content in respect of any outward objects. For summer being done, all things stand upon them with a weatherbeaten face, and the whole country, full of woods and thickets, represented a wild and savage hue.

I'm not sure what has brought me here on this dark and chilly afternoon, except it seemed like a promising place to gather some perspective at the end of another year, which also happens to be the end of the Second Millennium. From the pulloff beside Route 6 I have wandered out along the unraveling system of informal trails and have eventually circled out to the edge of the headland itself, some 50 feet above the land below me. The only bits of bright color are the vivid red-orange fruits of the winterberries, which glow like small fires in the swamps around Moon Pond below the bluffs.

High Head is a formation of some geological significance, for it represents the northern tip of glacial Cape Cod, deposits left by the last series of ice sheets that covered this land and withdrew some 15,000 to 18,000 years ago. As they retreated in the face of a warming climate, their melting caused the sea level to rise, and several thousand years ago ocean waves and currents began to erode this bluff and others along the outer edges of the Cape. Over the past six millennia much of this eroded material gradually formed everything I see before me: the curled-fist formation of dunes, wooded hills, and long, curving sand spits we know today as the Provincetown Hook.

I know this because of a geological theory that itself is only a little over a generation old, one developed largely from research conducted by the Cape's distinguished coastal geologist, Dr. Graham Giese, whose home is nearby. It is a theory, increasingly borne out by subsequent research, that adds another fascinating layer to the gradually evolving story of the Cape's geological formation, a story that continually adds new chapters in an ongoing process Henry Beston succinctly summed up in his maxim, "Creation is here and now."

But it is not the geological story that captures my attention this afternoon, fascinating as that is, as much as our own human story here on this ethereal extremity of the Cape, and how intimately entwined we have been in the creation of the landscape that surrounds me.

William Bradford's words are a useful benchmark for how much we have transformed this "unknown coast" over the past four centuries from a "hideous and desolate wilderness," a place of "little solace or content," to a place where, even at such a late date in the year, the traveler can easily find food, lodging and good cheer. Much of this human transformation is visible from High Head, even on such a dark afternoon as this: the dense, unbroken line of commercial development that stretches along Beach Point for over two miles; the broad four-lane thoroughfare of Route 6 itself; the instantly recognizable jumbled roofline of Provincetown clustered along the shore of its broad harbor; and the most prominent landmark of all, the tall, somber, stone tower of the Pilgrim Monument itself, blinking its two red aircraft warning lights like a pair of glowing eyes.

But much of the dramatic transformation of the scene before me is less obvious. It needs to be seen with the mind's eye, preferably from a place like this, where imagination can project knowledge out onto the land itself.

Imagine with me, if you will, that the slow, ongoing, incremental process of human and natural change here has suddenly ceased.

Time has stopped. Now it slowly begins to run in reverse, then gradually speeds up, creating a backward time-lapse movie of the scene before us. As we go back ten years or so, the new houses that have lately been sprouting up on the old railroad right-of-way begin to disappear like balloons popping. Going back 50 years, we see that Route 6 itself has disappeared, and only Route 6A, the old shore road, carries traffic into Provincetown. The railroad tracks have been restored along the right of way, and the old freight or "sand train" once again makes its way up to the Cape tip to haul sand to the mainland.

Now we are back a hundred years, watching the stone tower of the Monument unbuild itself in 1904, and frequent passenger trains bringing the first substantial crowds of summer tourists to Provincetown. All but a few of the oldest structures on Beach Point have vanished into the future. The pine woods behind us have vanished as well, and a rolling treeless plain stretches south down the curve of the Cape as far as we can see, giving us clear unobstructed views of the flashes of Highland and Nauset lights.

Now we have traveled a century and a half into the past. The shore road, as well as the earthen causeway that was built in 1872 to carry the first trains into Provincetown, are gone. The brackish shallow waters of Pilgrim Lake have been transformed into East Harbor, an open saltwater estuary where Yankee captains were said to have deliberately scuttled their boats to hide them from the British during the War of 1812. Foot travelers such as Thoreau, coming from up Cape, have to take the long circuitous sand road of the Old King's Highway around the back of East Harbor, through the dunes, to get to Provincetown.

Four hundred years ago now, and the visible settlement of Provincetown has disappeared, though a few Portuguese, Basque, and other fishing vessels are moored in its harbor, as they have been for at least a century before the Mayflower dropped anchor.

But what, we ask in surprise, has happened to the dunes — those ancient, wild, moving hills of sand? Well, it turns out they aren't so ancient after all, nor wild, for that matter. They were, in fact, the result of excessive woodcutting and pasturing of cattle during the eighteenth century. Now the famous "natural wonder" of the Provinceland dunes has reverted to thickly forested hills, described by one early explorer as "compassed about to the very sea with oaks, pines, juniper, sassafras, and other sweet wood." High Head itself has regained its original forest, and Pamet Indians pad softly along its trails, perhaps coming here to bury catches of corn for the coming winter.

Now let's speed up our journey into the past: 1000 years ago, 3000, 6000. We see the long curved spiral of Long Point begin to unwind and retract, like a piece of spaghetti into a mouth. Then the entire Provincetown Hook begins to grow thinner and shorten; from a curled fist it becomes a low, sandy stump, then a mere beach, then nothing. Open water laps at the base of High Head where we stand. Then, gradually, the waters begin to recede, sea level drops, and a flat open wet plain begins to emerge: the older, lower continental plain that underlies the Cape's glacial deposits.

Now, finally, 10,000 or 12,000 years ago, the climate has grown noticeably cooler. A June day feels more like this late November afternoon. Tiny arctic birch trees grow on a tundra landscape and in the distance caribou can be seen grazing. Far off to the north we make out a low white bank of clouds, growing gradually closer. As it does we see it is not clouds at all, but a river of ice flowing south, one that grows into an immense frozen wall of ice over a mile tall, crossing the plain toward us, gradually scooping up the sand, gravel, and boulders that it deposited during its last advance, sucking them back up into its white maw until at last it towers over us and the battlements of High Head like a gigantic breaking wave. . . .

Suddenly, this fantasy is broken by the appearance of a tall tree of lights on the horizon. It is the annual lighting of the Pilgrim Monument that takes place each year on this day, a tradition that transforms that somber, solid, dark tower into a seasonal beacon of hope and renewal, not unlike the bonfires Native Americans are said to have lit with the advent of the winter solstice. It signals to me that it is time to leave this solitary reverie and join my own kind for the festivities in town. I get up and wander back across the darkling moor to the car, but as I do I am aware of the ranks of pines, and behind them the darker, leafless oaks to the south, slowly encroaching on the moors. No fantasy these, but reality operating on a scale too slow for us to perceive with our senses alone, yet as persistent as the vanished past, waiting to reclaim the present.

DIRECTIONS

Heading north on Route 6 in North Truro, High Head Conservation Area is on the left, just a few hundred feet beyond the turnoff for the National Seashore's Pilgrim Spring Area on the right. It is unmarked, and no left turn is allowed here, so you will have to continue down the hill and take the first left turn off Route 6, turn around, and come back up the highway. Look for the small blue CONSERVATION AREA sign on the right and the pulloff parking area 1,000 feet ahead.

Bed of Memories.

NOT LONG AGO, ON A FINE SPRING DAY, I SET OFF on foot from Provincetown center to retrace a walk I first took four decades ago: along the old railroad bed that runs from Provincetown through Truro to the terminus of the Cape Cod Rail Trail in South Wellfleet. Although even then trains were long gone from the Cape-tip and the track had been torn up, the bed itself was still an unencumbered pathway, a wonderful cross section of the Lower Cape running through and beside woodland, dunes, open heathland, village centers, marshes, wetlands, and ponds.

Walking east through town, however, I discovered that the first part of the route of the railroad track had been totally transformed. It now runs through a private alley, a large parking lot, and Harry Kemp Way, a paved road lined with commercial and professional offices. In fact, over the course of my walk, I found that, except for those portions within the Cape Cod National Seashore, most of this once open footpath has now either been turned into paved roads and parking lots, obstructed with new houses built directly on the right of way, or completely obliterated by new developments. With it have gone a piece of the Cape's history, public access to some of its most spectacular landscapes, and a considerable amount of wildlife habitat.

But in the East End of Provincetown I came upon a pleasant surprise: beginning at Howland Street and stretching east almost a mile and a half is a relatively undisturbed and undeveloped section of the rail right of way. Here, flowing through thick woodland and shrub swamps, the old bed remains intact, and a gentle recovery of natural communities has taken place over the years since it last shook with the passage of the old "sand trains."

In this stretch I encountered again the same soft sand road I first walked in the spring of 1963. It was slow walking here, as it was on all the roads in Provincetown before they were paved. It's why wagon wheels in Provincetown had rims five inches wide. When Henry David Thoreau visited here in 1849, he even saw "a baby's wagon with tires six inches wide to keep it near the surface." I found myself dropping back into that flat-footed walk that one uses on soft sand, a practice that Thoreau said gave Provincetowners "a peculiar gait recognizable on the mainland, particularly among the women."

More than a half century after the last train entered Provincetown, the sand is still peppered with thousands of small cinders and pieces of charcoal, reminders of the old coal-burning locomotives that not only passed through these woods but also frequently set them on fire. Now a solid oak canopy has gently closed over the once open train track. Clumps of shadbush raise clouds of white blossoms beside the bed that recall the plumes of locomotive smoke that sifted through the woods. A series of narrow trails wind aimlessly off into the upland stands of pine and oak and around the perimeter of substantial stands of swamp white cedar trees. Once common

on the Cape and the original source of our ubiquitous white cedar shingles, swamp cedars are now a rare botanical community in most towns. Lovely stands of tupelo are just beginning to come out with their little spear-shaped green flames of leaves. Beneath them bloom diminutive starflowers and Canadian mayflowers, and early blue butterflies drift like bits of satin in the spring air.

Heading east, from Howland Street to Snail Road, the first section of this walking path is part of the town's Water Resource Protection District. Beyond Snail Road, however, one enters something unexpected and unique in Provincetown: the Foss Woods Conservation Area. The wonder of Foss Woods is not its size (it encompasses only 15 acres), or what it contains, but that it exists at all. In a town that has almost 80 percent of its land mass included within the Cape Cod National Seashore, one might expect open space purchases to be a hard sell. And they have been. In fact Foss Woods was the first piece of town conservation land ever acquired since Provincetown's incorporation in 1727.

Yet, in April of 1995, local voters overwhelmingly approved the purchase of Foss Woods at a cost of $425,000 (61 percent of which was reimbursed by the state grants and private donations). The acquisition was the result of a concerted effort by many organizations, including the local Save Foss Woods Committee, the Trust for Public Land, the Provincetown Conservation Commission, the executors of the Foss estate, and the Provincetown Conservation Trust.

Still, why would a community with a smaller land area than any other Cape town, known for its commercialism and its tenacity regarding private property rights, do such a thing?

At first glance, Foss Woods does not provide an obvious answer. To a visitor from off-Cape or one of the Upper Cape towns, Foss Woods appears as a rather ordinary, not particularly impressive stretch of your standard-variety, mixed pitch-pine-and-oak woodlands that are abundant in almost every Cape town. But Provincetown is not, and never has been, like "every Cape town," and one town's "ordinary woodland" may, in fact, be another's endangered habitat.

As Celine Gandolfo, who spearheaded the Save Foss Woods Committee, pointed out, "Only 12 percent of the land within the National Seashore in Provincetown is mature forest. Except for Foss

Woods, the rest of the town's old woodland is privately owned, and part of that gets cut down every day as the last remaining parcels in town are being developed." Records show that Foss Woods has been an undisturbed woodland for over 100 years, making it, by Provincetown standards, an "old-growth forest."

Perhaps a better way to view Foss Woods, and to understand its significance, is to look at an aerial photo or a topographical map of Provincetown. Here one sees that, lying between the dense street grid of Provincetown and the moving dunes of the Provincelands, is a thin green belt of woodlands, ponds, and wetlands stretching from Herring Cove on the west to Pilgrim Lake on the east. Most of this wooded belt is included within the protected confines of the National Seashore, but its eastern end lies inside the boundaries of the town. It is this section of woods and wetlands that comprises the Water Resource Protection District and Foss Woods. As such, it forms an important wildlife corridor between the harbor and the dunes, and a significant habitat for migratory and breeding songbirds, particularly warblers.

In addition, an environmental survey of Foss Woods found at least two state-listed "species of special concern": the Eastern box turtle, which has been in decline statewide for several decades and requires undisturbed woodland habitat to survive; and the highly unusual checkered rattlesnake plantain orchid, which has been found in only one other location on Cape Cod.

Because of its location, the stretch of railroad bed running through Foss Woods also has the potential to be a significant link in the ongoing Cape Cod Pathways project to link all fifteen Cape communities with walking trails.

Such significant environmental assets might seem sufficient argument for its preservation, but for the many local citizens who worked assiduously for its acquisition, Foss Woods has a value that goes beyond such strict ecological components. They were motivated in part by the desire to create some of their own open space, managed for and by Provincetowners, and to preserve for the enjoyment of future generations the traditional landscape and uses of their town. The National Seashore's Provincelands are for the nation, indeed for the world, but Foss Woods, though open to the public at large, remains a part of Provincetown. As one resident, Donna Joseph, put it: "When I was a girl, I would gather berries, nuts, and herbs in woodlands all over Provincetown. Now there are houses covering all of my old hunting grounds. We need to save Foss Woods for our children. You can't put a price tag on it."

This kind of proprietary sentiment fuels much of the movement to preserve local open spaces on Cape Cod, particularly smaller ones like Foss Woods. It seems to me a healthy and hopeful, even an essential sentiment. The creation of such large preserves as the Cape Cod National Seashore, Nickerson and South Beach State Parks, the Wellfleet and Ashumet Audubon Sanctuaries has been invaluable; but it has also inadvertently fostered a dangerous dichotomy, namely, the belief that there are two kinds of land: that which has been set aside for conservation and wildlife, and that which has not and is therefore open for any kind of human use and alteration.

On that spring day Foss Woods allowed me to recover a bit of my own past and a landscape I had encountered when I first lived on the Cape, as well as unexpected pieces of the Cape's older, almost vanished history. More importantly, though, Foss Woods is a shining example of how the spirit of local stewardship can flourish even in a town that might seem to have little reason to nurture it.

(Note: On April 13, 1999, Provincetown Town Meeting voters overwhelmingly approved $1.6 million for another significant purchase of local conservation land: 7.52 acres of upland surrounding Shankpainter Pond, a globally significant wetland containing 11 endangered species and the world's largest known quaking bog in a dune environment.)

DIRECTIONS

As you enter Provincetown on Route 6, take your first left at the intersection with Snail Road. The entrance to Foss Woods is on the left side a few hundred feet along, with parking on that side of Snail Road for five cars.

Managing to Survive.

AT 6:30 ON A JUNE MORNING THE FOG AT LONG

Point is quite thick. "Maushop's smoke," the old Indian legends

termed it, referring to the benevolent pipe-smoking giant of

Wampanoag creation stories. Visibility is perhaps 100 yards.

Although it is almost summer, the scene in front of me is still a

ghostly expanse of last year's bleached grass stems about 18 inches

high – little bluestem grass, the characteristic plant of this coastal

prairie. From the tops of the dead grass stems pouchy-lacey spider

webs hang like little ghost handkerchiefs that have been dropped

there overnight.

Out of the mist comes the sound of birdsong, mostly song sparrows but cloaked, like disembodied voices. To my right, also invisible, I hear the ghostly flapping of a cormorant taking off from the brackish waters of Tisbury Great Pond. A half-mile to the south, beyond the invisible line of dunes, the surf beats against the outer beach.

Long Point is a 636-acre sanctuary owned by The Trustees Of Reservations and encompasses a patchwork of oak woodland, pitch pine barrens, sandplain grassland, and heathland. It is these last two habitats that make this place environmentally special, for there are only a few square miles of coastal sandplain heath and grassland left on earth, most of it on the southern shores of Martha's Vineyard and Nantucket. A number of endangered plants and animals depend upon these habitats for continued existence. At least one species — the eastern prairie chicken — lost its fight for survival here when the last known individual, an old male, perished on Martha's Vineyard in 1932. Among those that remain are short-eared owls, northern harriers (marsh hawks), barrens buck moth, Gerard's underwing moth, purple tiger beetles, Nantucket shadbush (which exists only on Nantucket and Martha's Vineyard), sandplain blue-eyed grass, bushy rockrose, northern blazing star, and sandplain flax.

Although some of these species are difficult to find and identify, the beauty of Long Point Wildlife Refuge is astonishing and self-evident. Long Point itself, a rippling expanse of coastal prairie set between Long Cove and Tisbury Great Ponds, is dominated by grasses and flowers. There are patches of wild strawberry vines climbing up through bayberry, delicate four-petaled bluets on long stems, a small amaryllis known as yellow stargrass, pink sugar-candy clusters of sheep laurel, and the lovely light purple, six-petaled blossoms of sandplain blue-eyed grass. Tree swallows, which nest in abundance on the property, arc in and out of sight through the fog. There are signs of recent burns running through the grassland and stretching far to the northeast into oak woods. It's a ghost landscape this time of day, with this fog.

Last evening I sat on the porch of the staff house sipping wine with Chris Egan, the sanctuary's superintendent. The air was crystal clear, and I was struck by the rich, layered horizontality of this landscape: the grasslands and heathlands and shrublands in front of

us, shelving off to the wide, flat ponds on either side, and beyond it all the low, long line of dunes with a break here and there through which I could catch a glimpse of dark ocean.

Chris is a cheerful, forthcoming man in his mid-30s who, after eight years, seems still unable to get used to his good fortune of living here year round: "There's not many places in the Northeast where I can sit on my porch and look at this view," he said with understated satisfaction. This is his favorite time of day, when the visitors are gone, when the evening seems to settle, and in that quiet you begin to hear the sounds and the rhythms of the land — the swallows twittering back and forth, the *ch-caw* call from the ringneck pheasants that run in the brush, the distant sound of the surf, gulls calling over the water, two swans drifting slowly with statuesque immobility on Tisbury Great Pond. A barn owl is roosting in a big nesting box in back of the house, and an osprey perches on a tall pole to the northwest, like a presiding spirit of the place.

Chris had been talking about the long and complex history, human and natural, of Long Point, and the equally complex management program the sanctuary employs to maintain these globally endangered habitats and their extraordinary diversity of life:

CE: We know for certain that the Wampanoags used this area for hunting and fishing for centuries before the Europeans came. Long Cove Pond has some fairly extensive middens along its shore. They also cut the forests for firewood, boats, and other tools, and burned them for agriculture. John Brereton, who sailed by here in 1602, remarked on the number of meadows and cornfields he saw.

RF: So are you saying that the first inhabitants deliberately created these grasslands and heathlands?

CE: We don't know that for sure. But we know from our experience here that if you simply leave things alone, you get a succession habitat of pitch pine and scrub oak, and you lose diversity when that happens. Sometimes a major storm, like the 1938 hurricane, will cause a large dieback in the encroaching trees, but that doesn't happen often. Salt spray and poor soil near the shore certainly stress a lot of plants and retard the growth of oaks and other trees. But all the evidence suggests that fire and clearing were always major factors affecting the landscape of Long Point and similar areas. When Long Point and other parts of the south shore passed into the hands of the first white settlers, the landscape continued to be used for farming and grazing for the next two hundred fifty years. These grasslands in particular were used for sheep grazing, which helped to maintain the open, prairielike environment. Around 1900, much of the south shore was acquired by the then-popular hunting clubs, which used the area mostly for duck shooting and fishing. Long Point was acquired by the Tisbury Pond Club in 1912. The porch we're sitting on is part of the hunting lodge they built here, and the storage shed behind it is an old schoolhouse they moved here. The Pond Club didn't do much managing, but they had a caretaker who mowed every summer. In the middle of the last century the hunting clubs were disbanded, and the remaining members eventually gave the land to the Trustees as a sanctuary. The mowing was stopped for a few years, and then we began to explore using fire as a tool.

RF: You know, those of us who grew up in the fifties and sixties, listening to Smokey the Bear warning us, "Only you can prevent forest fires," were conditioned to think of fire as something uniformly destructive, to be suppressed at all costs. Why did you switch from mowing to fire as a management tool?

CE: For a number of reasons. When you mow a field right up to the edge of a woodland you get a strictly demarcated line, a square feel to an area. Two feet off of that field into the woods you get a whole different set of plants and animals. Instead of having clearly defined lines in the landscape, what we're trying to do is to overlap things, to create a softer transition between burned and nonburned areas. Fire provides a much more varied habitat than mowing, because it burns unevenly, hotter in some places than in others, allowing certain communities to persist and others to come in. Also, some areas, such as the grassland just across the road, are burned every two or three years, while that woodland beyond it won't be burned again for another ten years.

RF: So you burn the woodland as well as the grasslands?

CE: Yes. This burn unit actually goes all the way from the dunes north nearly a mile to the top of the trail system on the oak woods. North of the grassland we're burning under the oak canopy. We're not actually trying to take down all the trees, just thinning them out a bit using fire as a selective tool, allowing more trees to remain, but giving it more of a savanna feel. And then further north we're creating a section of forest that's a buffer area, a transition zone from savanna to woodland.

RF: You make it sound like a fairly precise science.

CE: No, not really. We're still in the research phases of it, but we believe we have a fairly decent understanding of fire effects. It's a much more subtle management tool than mowing. When you mow repeatedly, you create this homogenous landscape. When we use fire as a tool, especially when we get into successive treatments, the fire won't burn everything; it'll kind of burn through in patches. We don't know exactly how the fire will burn, and we don't really push it — we just let it go. We let the fire decide where to burn, within limits. Plus, we have a whole variety of techniques we're using, not just fire. The area on this side of Long Cove Pond is treated with fire only. On the east side of the pond, by the summer parking lot, we have an area where we're using a combination of mowing and burning. We're also exploring bringing animals back on this property as grazing tools. We're in negotiations with a local farmer to lease out his sheep and goats here this fall, and then just beyond that, on Homer Pond, is a control area. We're just letting that be — no mowing, burning, grazing, nothing down there. Once a year or once every other year, we do a fairly comprehensive survey of each of these areas to see how they're changing, what's going on. So we're really trying to map out and get some data from each of these techniques: fire is only one of them.

As the sun disappeared over the western dunes and dusk crept up onto the porch where we sat, I asked Chris what was his favorite time of year here.

"I guess I love it best in the autumn," he replied, "when the crowds are gone and the sun is setting and the grasses all turn red and the huckleberry and other heath plants turn brilliant vermilion." He paused, and then, as if afraid of tempting fate by appearing to boast of his good fortune, he added, "But you know, the great thing about this place is that even in the height of summer, when we get hundreds of visitors a day, it's easy to find solitude here. The summer parking is on the other side of Long Cove Pond and few people wander very far from it. You can always walk over to this side

DIRECTIONS

Mid-June through Mid-September:
Traveling west on the Edgartown–West Tisbury Road, proceed 0.3 mile beyond the main entrance to the Martha's Vineyard Airport. Turn left onto Waldron's Bottom Road and follow for 1.3 miles. Turn left onto Scrubby Neck Road (Path), then right onto Hughe's Thumb Road and follow signs for 1.2 miles to the summer parking area.

and find a place to be alone, to feel the rhythms and experience the tranquillity of this place."

The following morning, as I walk down the east side of the Loop Trail through the fog, I can see the varied evidence of the recent burns. Some areas, which apparently burned quite hot, remain completely black. Others, not so deeply burned, already have green huckleberry and blueberry shoots coming up. (Fire, Chris told me, also releases mineral soils, which many of the endangered plant species need to germinate.) This mix of open habitat reflects the mixed use of the earliest inhabitants of this land, the Wampanoags. Because of the fog there is no sign of man visible except for this sand track I'm following, so that it's easy to imagine myself back 400 years.

Suddenly the track becomes soft and yielding underfoot as I reach the long and shallow backslope of the dune coming to the ocean. A myriad of tiny blossoms of golden heather cast a golden haze across the dunes, splashed by the garish pastels of the beach roses. If it were clear, I might see a short-eared owl and harriers hunting this time of the day. In the winter, Chris said, he often sees snowy owls and occasional bald eagles out on these dunes.

When I come through a break in the dunes onto the shore, I am surprised at the size of the surf here, much bigger than on the Cape's south shore. Chris told me that erosion is taking place here at a rate of about 10 feet a year, a very rapid rate compared to the more resistant morainal deposits to the north and west. "Due to the very soft sandplain composition of the deposits on the Vineyard's south shore," he said, "the ocean is gradually hollowing out the Vineyard, turning it from a pork chop shape into more of a horse-shoe."

Within living memory, he said, Long Pond was an arm of Tisbury Great Pond and was called Long Cove. Long Point, then, was actually a "point" in a single pond. But gradually the beach has retreated and separated the two. "We have aerial photographs from the 1950s and it's pretty dramatic how far the ocean has advanced since then."

I come off the beach through a little break in the dunes onto the southern shore of Tisbury Great Pond, whose still, shallow waters

Mid-September to Mid-June:
Traveling west on the Edgartown–West Tisbury Road, proceed 1.1 miles beyond the main entrance to the Martha's Vineyard Airport. Turn left onto Deep Bottom Road and follow for 1.5 miles, always bearing left at forks. Turn right onto Thumb Point Road (refuge signs at inter-section) and follow for 1.3 miles to the off-season parking lot.

remain mostly hidden in the fog. A single quawk, or black-crowned night heron, flies overhead and lands at the edge of the pond, standing there and waiting with infinite patience. "In the wintertime," Chris said, "we get seals hauling out here quite often, mostly harbor seals, some greys. They're usually here only when the ponds open to the ocean because there's a lot of food that comes out of this pond, that gets pulled out by the tides — fish, oysters, crabs, perch. The seals will even come into the ponds then. But the best thing is to see river otters playing on the ice in winter. They run and slide over the ice — it's obvious they're just having a great time."

The west side of the Loop Trail has much more shrubby growth: lots of bayberry, some scrub oak, huckleberry, blueberry, shadbush, and beach plum. I spot a couple of rare sandplain blue-eyed irises in the low places. Redwings and yellowthroats call along the pond edges, and some towhees answer from out of the woods to the north. Up ahead, out of the fog, the outline of Chris's house begins to take shape like the ghost of the future.

An Unnatural Treasure, or, How We Became Sheep.

THE "MOORS" OF NANTUCKET, AS THEY ARE

locally known, are generally regarded as the heart of Nantucket, its

very essence, its soul. More than any other aspect of this remarkable

island, they are what makes Nantucket Nantucket, the most distinc-

tive natural feature of its landscape.

There are only three problems with this concept: (1) the "moors" are

not really moors; (2) they are not natural; and (3) many of the

moors aren't even "moors" anymore.

The first problem is something of a botanist's quibble. True moors are usually stretches of high open land with poorly drained soils and peat bogs, characterized by heather, such as the moors of Scotland and Devon. The Nantucket moors are technically coastal heathland and sandplain grassland, dominated by such species as lowbush blueberry, huckleberry, bayberry, little bluestem, bearberry, poverty grass, asters, and goldenrod.

Moreover, Nantucket's moors represent one of the more dramatic examples of human alteration of the natural landscape. Like many parts of the Cape and Islands, the original forests of Nantucket were cleared by European settlers for fields and pastures in the late seventeenth century. By the mid-1800s some 15,000 sheep were grazing the hills and outwash plains of the island, creating the characteristic "moor" landscape that has become so deeply imbedded in the idea of Nantucket.

Finally, with the abandonment of most agriculture in the early twentieth century, the moors have been increasingly invaded by woody plants such as scrub oak, pitch pine and viburnum, so that hundreds of acres of former moorland have become nearly impenetrable tangles of shrubs and stunted trees.

This last development has led to an interesting environmental conundrum, to one of the more ambitious experiments in land management, and to a unique partnership of conservation and private organizations. Although most of the coastal heathland and sandplain grassland on Nantucket are technically artificial, manmade environments, they represent an important and globally scarce habitat for such rare and endangered species as the short-eared owl, northern harrier, or marsh hawk, bushy rockrose, broom crowberry, and Nantucket shadbush. The Nantucket Conservation Foundation estimates that over 90 percent of the worldwide acreage of sandplain grassland exists on Nantucket, Tuckernuck, and Martha's Vineyard, with most of it on Nantucket.

In the early 1980s, the Foundation, the Nantucket Heathlands Partnership, and the Massachusetts Audubon Society conducted experiments in brush cutting and controlled burning as a means of preserving and restoring these habitats. Although the experiments showed promise, funding and manpower were lacking to apply these procedures on a broad scale. Then, in 1996, an innovative agreement was reached between these organizations, the Commonwealth's

Natural Heritage and Endangered Species Program, and the Nantucket Golf Club. In exchange for the state's permission to develop a new golf course in Siasconset, the golf club agreed to provide funding for the restoration and management of abutting conservation land. This association was named the Partnership for Harrier Habitat Preservation (PHHP), after one of the protected species, and has achieved the reversal of woody succession on hundreds of acres of former grassland and heath. (It seems appropriate that one of the rare plants being protected by golf money is St. Andrew's Cross, which shares its name with the famous course of the Royal and Ancient Golf Club in Scotland.)

The core of this unique landscape is Middle Moors, an area of more than 2000 acres owned by the Nantucket Conservation Foundation, lying between Polpis Road on the north and Milestone Road on the south. I visited Middle Moors in October on the week after Columbus Day, when the crowds are gone and rates go down. It was an almost perfect autumn day, clear skies, light winds from the north, temperatures in the low 60s.

I began my walk at Altar Rock, an island landmark that sits on the spine of Nantucket's glacial terminal moraine at the northern edge of the moors. At 100 feet above sea level, Altar Rock is not the highest point on Nantucket — that modest honor belongs to Folger Hill (108 feet) to the east — but it does provide a spectacular and panoramic overlook of the moors. (Nantucketers, making the most out of what they have, like to sport bumper stickers that urge you to "SKI ALTAR ROCK.") Here the modest hills and valleys of the moraine gradually spread out into the low, flat outwash plains to the south. The moraine, with its heavier soils, supports most of the heathland, while the sandier, drier soils of the plains contain most of the grassland.

An interesting paradox of Nantucket is that although over 13,000 acres, or almost 45 percent of the island, have been protected as conservation land, the flat and open nature of its landscape makes the effects of development and environmental degradation more obvious than in most places. On the northern edge of the Middle Moors, for instance, several mega-trophy homes have reared their towers and cantilevered decks in recent years. Some of them are architecturally attractive, superbly built with traditional materials, and so on — but monstrously out of scale to this diminutive and open terrain. Cars and the omnipresent rental scooters are limited by posted Foundation regulations to "well-established roadways" in the moors, but an intricate spider web of meandering roads and trails radiates to the south, scarring the landscape. Only a few vehicle passes can mark a swath of heath for decades, and it is difficult to supervise such a vast area.

I walked west on one of the sand roads into the Shawkemo Hills, a sea of gently undulating terrain, largely covered with rounded domes of scrub oak, some jagged thrusts of red cedar hung with bright red banners of poison ivy and Virginia creeper, and open patches of fiery blueberry and bearberry.

Then, as if suddenly materializing out of nowhere, four whitetail deer stood right in the road, staring at me: a large doe and three smaller yearlings. They took off up the road, high-tailing it, as it were, waving their eponymous tails as if to say, "Come get me." They moved with that casual, slow, linked, syncopated movement deer have — one part of the body following another like links of chain. After 50 yards or so the mother stopped while the young ones disappeared into the shrubbery. Then, with an exuberant leap, she seemed to fly over the bordering shrubs and disappeared into the sea of green. Deer, at least, seem to have benefited from the cover provided by the regrowth of shrubs and low trees on the moors.

I turned south and headed towards the Pout Ponds, two of many small, shallow, kettle ponds that dot these moorlands. The slopes here are covered with large stands of blueberry and huckleberry. Now, in the low October sun, their leaves were backlit and seemed to glow, like stained glass, with the slanted light shining through it. The huckleberry leaves sported a dramatic combination of red and green, creating a hillside of pied beauty.

I came to the first pond on the left, a Lilliputian puddle barely 25 feet across with a tiny island at its south end. The surface was nearly covered with water lilies and fringed with rushes and sedges. Late-season pairs of red damselflies swung out over its waters, copulating on the wing. The pond is ringed with stands of bayberry the size of small trees. These shrubs seem to reach their peak size on these southern, windswept islands. (For a vivid illustration of the changes that have taken place in these moors over the past century, see if you can locate a copy of Peter Dunwiddie's fascinating book, *Changing Landscapes: A Pictorial Field Guide to a Century of Change on Nantucket*, published by the Nantucket Conservation Foundation in

1992. The book contrasts historic pictures of landscape features with their present-day appearance. The Pout Ponds photo from 1906, for instance, shows a nearly unbroken expanse of bluestem grass, bearberry, and other low heath plants. Only a few of the higher shrubs that now dominate are visible.)

Nantucket originally belonged to New York. I remember reading somewhere that when the island was ceded to Massachusetts, the ponds remained in New York ownership, and that therefore Massachusetts fishing licenses are not required to fish in Nantucket ponds. It is probably an apocryphal story, which is why I have not tracked down its authenticity. I like to think I might encounter men in Armani suits with fishing rods, standing at the edges of these small, hidden ponds, growling, "Youlookinatme? Fuggedaboudit!"

South of the Pout Ponds, entering an outwash valley, I encountered the first signs of active management: narrow mowed borders on one side of the road. There were also patches of little bluestem, its cottony seed heads and thin brown stems waving in the wind. It is clear that the mowing is already beginning to create continuities between these separated remnants of grassland.

At a crossroad I took one of the main moorland roads – Bernard Valley Road – east toward Gibbs Pond. Here, in the outwash plain, the land is much flatter and open. The roads here are nearly pure sand, not full of little stones and pebbles as they were in the moraine. Large areas of *Hudsonia,* or poverty grass, lined the road-sides, little green rag-mop tufts of both the more common beach heather and the rarer golden heather.

It was here, in March 2002, just north of Bernard Valley Road, that some 30 acres of pitch pine and scrub oak were set ablaze in a controlled burn by the PHHP. Sheets of flame and clouds of black smoke rose into the air like a miniature prairie fire. Although fire, in general, works best as a maintenance tool where the grassland is already established, burning woody areas helps to eliminate accumulated litter that might cause wildfires and also releases nutrients that encourage the growth of grasses.

Although the PHHP now actively manages some 350 acres of the Middle Moors, most burns are on a fairly small scale. Jim Lantowski, executive director of the Nantucket Conservation Trust, explained why they don't do more extensive burning. "Part of the problem is just getting a fire crew together. It takes a lot of work to get one of these burns going and kept under control, and we just don't have the manpower to do large burns. Also, you can't do large, Western-type burnings in the middle of what is essentially a residential suburb. It's just not practical. You can do small ones, but people get very worried if they see large fires."

I walked for nearly a mile east along this valley road. Now, in the heart of the Middle Moors, on this perfect autumn day, there were no signs of houses or other buildings, no vehicles, no one in sight — only the occasional drone of a small plane overhead. I felt as if on the next turn in the road I might meet a character out of a Thomas Hardy novel set on the Great Heath — Diggory Venn, perhaps.

Then, off to my right, the land opened up dramatically into a wide, nearly flat plain stretching over a half-mile south to a line of trees bordering Milestone Road. This, I thought, is what I had come to see. This is the face of Nantucket 150 years ago, or, as Herman Melville hyperbolically described it, "a mere hillock, and elbow of sand . . . [where] one blade of grass makes an oasis, three blades in a day's walk a prairie."

This was no prairie, however, but rather a recently mowed forest, a vast low mat of cut stumps, stems, and vines. Some 300 acres of woody growth had been mowed and grubbed out here the previous spring. Looking more closely, I saw blueberry, huckleberry, and even some scrub oak leaves growing from their cut stems. A few scattered trees had been left, apparently to provide scale, something to measure this measureless rolling plain against. It gave the landscape the effect of an African veldt with scattered thorn trees. But these were mostly Nantucket shad, thin, muscular trunks nearly 20 feet high.

One mowing does not a prairie make. The twisted oak stumps possess a stubbornness that will make them sprout again next spring, and the next. But if the botanists are correct, and repeated mowings and controlled burns are maintained, this landscape will one day become an eastern prairie again, home to owls, hawks, and grass-nesting birds. A true sandplain grassland will return, with New England blazing star, bushy rockrose, eastern silvery aster, and other prairie flowers blooming among grass emergent, bending in the wind.

And we will have become the sheep of the future.

DIRECTIONS

Coming from Nantucket center, take Polpis Road east toward Quaise. In approximately 2 miles look for the Life Saving Station Museum on the left. When you are 0.6 mile beyond the museum, and directly opposite Quaise Road, take the unmarked dirt road on the right. This is Altar Rock Road. Just a little way in you will see two small parking areas and a Nantucket Conservation Foundation sign. Park here and walk south to the summit of Altar Rock. Wander the open landscape and its labyrinth of dirt roads for hours.

For Further Information

Where guides to specific areas are available, they are mentioned in the text. For further information, scheduled field walks, or guides to additional areas, the following town offices and private organizations may be contacted. Information about most local land trusts and their holdings may be found at the Compact of Cape Cod Conservation Trusts Web site: www.compact.cape.com.

BARNSTABLE

Barnstable Conservation Commission, 367 Main Street, Hyannis, MA 02601; 508-362-4093.

Barnstable Land Trust, P.O. Box 226, Cotuit, MA 02635; 508-771-2585.

Cape Cod Pathways Project, Cape Cod Commission, P.O. Box 226, 3225 Main Street, Barnstable, MA 02630; 508-362-3828, ext. 350.

The Compact of Cape Cod Conservation Trusts, 3179 Main Street, P.O. Box 7, Barnstable, MA 02630; 508-362-2565; e-mail: compactr@cape.com.

Orenda Wildlife Land Trust, Box 669, West Barnstable, MA 02668; 508-362-4798.

Sandy Neck Rangers, 508-790-6345.

BOURNE

Bourne Conservation Commission, 24 Perry Avenue, Bourne, MA 02532; 508-759-6025.

Bourne Conservation Trust, 1104 Route 28A, Cataumet, MA 02534; 508-563-2800.

Army Corps of Engineers Field Office, Box 155, Buzzards Bay, MA 02532; 508-759-4431.

BREWSTER

Brewster Conservation Commission, 2198 Main Street, Brewster, MA 02631; 508-896-3701, ext. 135.

Brewster Conservation Trust, P.O. Box 268, Brewster, MA 02631.

Cape Cod Museum of Natural History, Route 6A, Brewster, MA 02631; 508-896-3867.

CHATHAM

Department of Planning and Development, 261 George Ryder Road, Chatham, MA 02633; 508-945-5168.

Chatham Conservation Foundation, Inc., 104 Crowell Road, Chatham, MA 02633; 508-945-4084.

DENNIS

Dennis Conservation Commission, 485 Main Street, South Dennis, MA 02660; 508-760-6123.

Dennis Conservation Trust, (contact: Richard A. Johnston, Hale and Dorr, 60 State Street, Boston, MA 02105; 617-526-6282).

EASTHAM

Eastham Natural Resources Department, Old Orchard Road, Eastham, MA 02642; 508-240-5972.

Eastham Conservation Trust, P. O. Box 183, Eastham, MA 02642; 508-255-5716; e-mail: lindh@c4.net.

FALMOUTH

Falmouth Conservation Commission, 59 Town Hall Square, Falmouth, MA 02540; 508-495-7445.

The 300 Committee, 157 Locust Street, Falmouth, MA 02540; 508-540-6759; e-mail: pdwyer@cape.com.

Salt Pond Areas Bird Sanctuaries, Inc., 881 Palmer Avenue, Falmouth, MA 02540; 508-548-8484; e-mail, spabsfal@aol.com.

HARWICH

Harwich Conservation Commission, 732 Main Street, Harwich, MA 02645; 508-430-7538.

Harwich Conservation Trust, 6 Freeman Street, Harwichport, MA 02646; 508-432-3997.

MASHPEE

Friends of the Mashpee National Wildlife Refuge, P.O. Box 1283, Mashpee, MA 02649; 508-495-1702.

Mashpee Conservation Commission, Town Hall, 16 Great Neck Road, Mashpee, MA 02649; 508-539-1400.

Mashpee Watershed and Land Trust, P.O. Box 1978, Mashpee, MA 02649; 508-539-2641.

The Trustees Of Reservations, Mashpee River Reservation; 781-740-7233.

ORLEANS

Orleans Conservation Commission, Town Hall, School Road, Orleans, MA 02653; 508-240-3700.

Orleans Conservation Trust, 51 Main Street, Orleans, MA 02653;
508-255-0183.

Orleans Supporters of Open Space, P.O. Box 2162, Orleans, MA 02653.

PROVINCETOWN

Provincetown Conservation Commission, Town Hall, Provincetown, MA
02657; 508-487-7000.

SANDWICH

Sandwich Conservation Commission, 16 Jan Sebastian Drive, Sandwich,
MA 02563; 508-888-4200.

Green Briar Nature Center, Discovery Hill Road, East Sandwich, MA
02537; 508-888-6870.

WELLFLEET

Wellfleet Conservation Commission, Town Hall, 300 Main Street,
Wellfleet, MA 02667; 508-349-0300.

Wellfleet Conservation Trust, P.O. Box 84, Wellfleet, MA 02667;
508-349-1434.

TRURO

Truro Conservation Commission, Town Hall Road, Truro, MA 02666.

Truro Conservation Trust, (contact: Ansel Chaplin, P.O. Box 340,
Orleans, MA 02653; 508-255-6300).

YARMOUTH

Yarmouth Natural Resource Department, 538 Forest Road, South
Yarmouth 02664; 508-760-4800.

Yarmouth Conservation Trust, P.O. Box 376, Yarmouth Port, MA 02675;
508-362-8270.

MARTHA'S VINEYARD

The Trustees of Reservations, Islands Regional Office, P.O. Box 2106,
The Wakeman Center, Vineyard Haven, MA 02568-2106; 508-693-7662;
e-mail: islands@ttor.org.

Martha's Vineyard Land Bank Commission, 167 Main Street, P.O. Box
2057, Edgartown, MA 02539; 508-627-7141.

NANTUCKET

Nantucket Conservation Foundation, P.O. Box 13, Nantucket, MA
02554; 508-228-2884; Web site: www.nantucketconservation.org.

Nantucket Land Bank Commission, 22 Broad Street, Nantucket, MA
02554; 508-228-7240.